Recovering from Church
and
Discovering Jesus

A Twelve-Step Program

Gerri Harvill
and
Stan Norman

ISBN 978-1-64140-850-9 (paperback)
ISBN 978-1-64140-851-6 (digital)

Christian Faith Publishing, Inc.
832 Park Avenue
Meadville, PA 16335
www.christianfaithpublishing.com

Step Titles are from *Step12.com*
Parts are adapted from subdivisions in *Breathing Under Water: Spirituality and the Twelve Steps* by Richard Rohr

Printed in the United States of America

For the women and men of
follow community and *Sandpoint Lifetree Café*,
fellow pilgrims on the journey.

Contents

Contents

Introduction

"I do not believe that such groups as Alcoholics Anonymous
are perfect any more than anything human is perfect, but
I believe what goes on in them is far closer to what Christ
meant his church to be, and what it originally was, than
much of what goes on in most churches I know."
—Frederick Buechner

Gerri's Story

Like an addict needing to be in recovery, be it from substance abuse
or a variety of other addictive behaviors, I had finally hit rock bottom. There was nowhere to go except up. It was time to figure it out
and do something about it. I needed to rid myself of my attachment
to that which held no meaning and provided no joy or avenue for
transformative change. I yearned to live a life closer to God, to actually follow Jesus by living like Jesus lived.

I had found the "church," and myself, to be addicted to rules,
rituals, and traditions. I was drowning in them, in fact. Unspoken
rules that excluded others, the very others that Jesus included.
Unexplained rituals that had come to have little or no meaning other
than "We've always done it that way." Traditions that were … well,
just that, traditions that seemed to satisfy the sentimental "Hallmark"
culture rather than provide avenues for transforming culture or making disciples of Jesus.

As I pondered this "once and done" Sunday morning worship that was passing as a spiritual life centered on Jesus, I came to see that what I was doing on Sunday morning was "playing church" and that the community around me was also engaged in this production. The denomination or "flavor" of worship service I attended or led didn't seem to change the situation. Tweaking the music, the pastors' attire, the style of worship, or the addition of a coffee bar did nothing to bring me closer to God or to others. One day I was just "DONE"![1]

Would I be able to give up the institutional church's Sunday morning worship service—the rules, the rituals, and the traditions—to actually pursue a life of following Jesus? What would that look like?

Being DONE with the traditional church, I was in no way DONE with God. It seemed that I had several options.

Option no. 1: Stay and work on "me": refocus my personal spiritual disciplines, reengage in the "mission field," and intensify my study of scripture. Pray that others would join me, collaborate, and commit to actually following Jesus daily, rather than just worshipping him on Sunday morning. However, after thirty years of being part of the local church, both as parishioner and pastor, I knew that if I stayed, my spirit would die.

Option no. 2: Leave the institutional "church" and with it any form of worship, spiritual learning, or community and just concentrate on reading the Bible, sitting with God, and being a "good" person. Be a hermit. However, I believe that Jesus calls us to community, that there are no solitary Christians. With James 2, "faith without works is dead," ringing in my ears and heart, this did not seem a viable way to live, or do as Jesus commanded, and go make disciples.

Option no. 3: Re-commit to being part of a community intent of living as Jesus lived, a community that embodied the lifestyle of the Acts 2 church. Re-commit to being a follower of Jesus intent on making disciples of him. This would mean being instrumental in the teaching and leading of such a community where none existed. Matthew 28, The Great Commission, "go and make disciples" began to mean simply going next door, or down the street. It meant going into the coffee shops and taverns and relating to others as Jesus did.

Sounds good! I choose option no. 3!

Great! BUT … I admit that I was addicted to the rules, rituals, and traditions of the institutional "church." How would I break away? What would I do on Sunday morning? How would I incorporate a real Sabbath into my weekly routine? What would this new community look like? Who would be attracted to this way of life?

Panic set in. I was at rock bottom. Desperate to leave and unable to stay.

How was I to move beyond this addiction to a lifestyle that served no one—not those outside of the church walls, pretty much not even those inside the church walls, and certainly not God?

When it comes to addiction recovery, no one does it better than the twelve-step programs. Could those programs guide those of us addicted to traditional, institutional church to recovery? What would that look like?

Stan's Story

Called to serve and called to lead others in serving, I've known my "calling" since junior high. But it's taken me almost fifty years to understand who and how I'm called to serve and lead.

I confess, my ego made me into an idealist. When an idealist is confronted with reality, they immediately try to recreate the reality in their own ideal. Here's how that played out for an overachiever like me.

When I was a sophomore at the US Coast Guard Academy, my tactics officer (a military mentor) took me aside to warn me that, while he appreciated my ridiculously high standards for personal performance and integrity, not everyone would. My immediate reaction was, "Why not? If I can meet those standards, so can they!"

I had a great twenty-two-year career in the Coast Guard. I even got to serve as commanding officer of two ships. About halfway into that career, I felt another call … a call to make admiral and to become chief of personnel so that I could make life better for the enlisted personnel (the worker bees in the Coast Guard). It was a noble call and an honorable goal. Every good leader knows how vital it is to take care of the people he or she leads. If the rules and regulations that protect the institution place an unnecessary burden on the people, those rules need to go. Needless to say, Coast Guard rule-followers did not appreciate my attitude. I didn't even achieve the rank of captain, let alone admiral! My pride and self-confidence had convinced me that I could change the Coast Guard from the inside out and from the top down.

Years later, as I went through the process of becoming an ordained pastor, I was asked to explain the difference between being captain of a ship and pastor of a church … not an unreasonable question. I responded that I thought there was really little difference: the goal was to bring the crew home alive while accomplishing the mission. As I reflected on the first few years that I served as a pastor, I realized that I was trying to do the same thing that I had tried to do in the Coast Guard. This time, I was trying to change the church from the inside out and from the top down. Jesus created his church to make disciples and transform the world. If institutional rules got in the way of making disciples and transforming the world then those rules had to go.

Here's the thing: I have always known that I was called to serve and lead. I thought that I was called to change institutions from the inside out and from the top down. I thought that I was called to rise high enough in the institution (Coast Guard and/or church) to be able to inspire and, if necessary, mandate change. I thought… well, you can see where this is going…not everyone I worked for, not everyone I worked with, wanted to change. In fact, some hated me just for suggesting that they needed to change.

Several years ago, God decided to create a "significant emotional event" in my life to get my attention off myself and what I could achieve through my own strength. The church where I served as one of the pastors had experienced slow but steady growth for three years. Then growth and giving topped-out and began a gradual decline. I realized that we had achieved our "market share" and that any further growth would have to come through engagement of the un-churched people in the community around us. Our need to become a more outwardly focused church was so obvious to the pastors that we didn't initially see the minefield we were walking into.

Things got ugly real fast! The "ruling class" was unwilling to change any rules or rituals to accommodate new people and fresh ideas. The pastors were accused of "liking the new people more than the long-time members." New outreach ministries were refused financial support. The pastors were personally attacked for trying new worship styles. There's a notebook in my office labeled "2012—The Year of Discontent."

I woke up one morning to the realization that I could not make the people in the church care or make them willing to change. I suppose that I'm either a glutton for punishment or a slow learner … or both. A faithful few of us hung on for three long years, but we just got worn out by the bickering, complaining, and gossiping. By December 2015, it became apparent to even this idealist, that the institutional church was not about to allow itself to be changed from the inside out.

I've read the gospels a hundred times, and it was there all along: Jesus was an outsider, a revolutionary, a radical. Dottie Escobedo-Frank says that "Change does not happen from the center. It happens, almost every time, from the edge."[2] Jesus came to change the world from the outside in, starting with the institution of the church.

In his landmark novel on Christian spirituality, *The Shack*, William P. Young records this conversation between Jesus and Mack (representing humanity):

> "As well-intentioned as it might be, you
> know that religious machinery can chew up peo-

ple!" Jesus said with a bite of his own, "An awful lot of what is done in my name has nothing to do with me and is often, even if unintentional, very contrary to my purposes."

"You're not too fond of religion and institutions?" Mack said, not sure if he was asking a question or making an observation.

"I don't create institutions—never have, never will."

After more than fifty years of trying to lead large institutions to embrace change, I'm DONE! My new chain of command is very simple: I follow Jesus. As simple as that sounds, it's not easy. I'm still addicted to rules and rituals and routines. Could my friends in the recovery community have found a way to guide and simplify this life journey?

Our Story

Let's get this out of the way right now. We are married, but not to each other.

After three years as sole pastor of a small rural church in Southwest Washington, Stan was reassigned to a slightly larger church in North Idaho, again as sole pastor. Two previous pastors of the Idaho church had identified a woman in the congregation named Gerri as a strong candidate for pastoral ministry. Stan challenged and encouraged Gerri to follow her call into pastoral ministry. In a few years, Gerri advanced from lay speaker to certified lay minister and finally to licensed local pastor.

Gerri has an insatiable desire to learn and know at the deepest levels. She is very discerning and contemplative—with a passion for music and art, poetry, and literature. Stan has degrees from the finest colleges and seminaries. He is a person of action and accomplishment, highly organized and driven. Our gifts are different, but complementary. We worked side by side for several years and it gradually became evident that we were more effective working as a team of equals.

We abandoned the institutional labels of "senior pastor" and "associate pastor" and became simply co-pastors. We also felt that the church, the community, and the culture needed to experience men and women working and leading together as equals. Jesus always sent his followers out two by two because he knew that in God's new math, one plus one always equals more than two. Team ministry is part of our calling and our passion.

We also share an overwhelming need to follow Jesus, no matter where that leads us. Jesus is leading us away from the institutional church, away from counting butts in pews and dollars in offering plates, away from rules and rituals that only serve to protect the institution at the expense of those Jesus loves.

This Book

The effectiveness of the twelve-step programs used by the substance abuse recovery community for spiritual formation has been recognized by several respected scholars, theologians, and church "experts," including Richard Rohr[3] and Rebekah Simon-Peter.[4] Rebekah Simon-Peter's blog in June 2015 led to our sermon series called "Church in Recovery" at the church we were serving during the months of July and August 2015.

We have experienced the spirituality of twelve-step programs for ourselves in almost a decade of working directly with Alcoholics Anonymous and Narcotics Anonymous groups.

This book is our attempt to apply the principles, techniques, and processes of the twelve-step programs to help those who are attempting to recover from addictions to institutional church and consumer religion (the DONES). We are Jesus-followers, so this book is written from a Christian perspective, but the steps may well be applied to other religious and political addictions. Even if you are not a "churchaholic," even if you are "spiritual, but not religious," we believe this book offers a proven path to spiritual formation and growth. Let us begin …

Hi, I'm Gerri!
Hi, I'm Stan!
We're churchaholics!

"In the beginning, the church was a fellowship of men and women centering on the living Christ. Then the church moved to Greece, where it became a philosophy. Then it moved to Rome, where it became an institution. Next it moved to Europe where it became a culture, and finally it moved to America, where it became an enterprise" (Richard Halverson, former chaplain to the United States Senate).

"Faith itself sometimes needs to be stripped of its social and historical encrustations and returned to its first, churchless incarnation in the human heart" (Christian Wiman).

Endnotes

1. "Dones" are the 65+ million people in the US who are DONE with the institutional church and the 7+ million who are almost done (Josh Packard and Ashley Hope, *Church Refugees*, Group Publishing, Loveland CO, 2015).
2. Dottie Escobedo-Frank and Rudy Rasmus, *Jesus Insurgency: The Church Revolution from the Edge*, Abingdon Press, Nashville, 2011, page 89.
3. Richard Rohr. *Breathing Under Water: Spirituality and the Twelve Steps*. St. Anthony Messenger Press, 2011 (Kindle).
4. Rebekah Simon-Peter. *15 Things AA Can Teach the Church*, rebekahsimonpeter.com/blog, June 13, 2015.

Part 1

God and Recovery

We suffer to get well.
We surrender to win.
We die to live.
We give it away to keep it.

—Richard Rohr
Breathing Under Water

Step 1

I Can't

We admitted we were powerless to change the church—that our lives within the church had become unspiritual.

In the recovery community of Alcoholics Anonymous, the original twelve-step program for recovering from addiction, this step reads: "We admitted we were powerless over alcohol—that our lives had become unmanageable."[1] We have contextualized it for our particular addiction.

This admission, or confession, is the critical first step in overcoming any addiction. As long as we continue to insist that we are in charge, that we are in control, that we have the willpower to make the changes that we need to make; we will continue to allow our addiction to control us. This is not a self-help program!

The "Americanization" of Christianity has made this a particularly tough step for most churchaholics in the United States. The "common good" has been displaced by individual freedoms, Jesus-centered living has been displaced by self-centered living, service to others has been displaced by consumerism, giving the poor "a hand up" has been displaced by the notion of wealth "trickling down." In the church, the "ministry of all believers" has been displaced by professional clergy who are viewed as hired hands, and, of necessity, are more focused on their careers than on their call from God to lead the church. The church that was intended to transform the culture has been transformed by the culture; pulpits (power) and paychecks (wealth) have displaced disciple-making and community engagement as the institutional church's mission.

The very foundation of any relationship with God is the acknowledgment that we are not God, that we are unable to control every aspect of our lives, that we are broken. During a church meeting at one of the churches where Stan served as pastor, a woman who was a respected leader in the community and the church exclaimed, "We're not broken! You don't need to fix us!" Like so many members of the Christian church in the West, this woman was so frightened at the prospect of changing that she became defensive at the very suggestion that changes to the rules and rituals that she had grown up with were necessary. If we're not broken, what do we need God or Jesus for? In his letter to the first Jesus-followers in Rome, the Apostle Paul says, "Everyone has sinned; we all fall short of God's glorious standard" (Romans 3:23, New Living Translation, Jesus-Centered Bible).

In our context, we DONES must first admit that we are powerless to change the institutional church. We have to confess that the rules, rituals, and traditions of the institution will not restore our spirit or repair our broken relationship with God. The Pharisees tried to restore the Israelites' relationship with God by strict adherence to every letter of every law in the Hebrew Bible (our Old Testament). In fact, they added a few rules of their own just to be on the safe side.

We, too, have added rules. Our culture has a long list of what tasks need to be done within the worshipping community, as well as in social, economic, and political situations. We worry about who is qualified, or not, to do those tasks, where, and how. It didn't work for the Pharisees in the first century, and it won't work for us in the twenty-first century.

When we are focused on rule-keeping, there is no room for imagination. There is no room for listening to God. There is no room for the Spirit of God to work. There is no room for God in our already-too-busy lives. God is interested in the Spirit of the Law, not the letter of the law. Jesus said, "God is Spirit, so those who worship him must worship in spirit and in truth" (John 4:24, NLT, Jesus-Centered Bible).

No More Tweaking

In October 2015, we attended the Third Annual Future of the Church Summit at Group Publishing in Loveland, Colorado. About 130 Christian church leaders, more than half of whom were pastors, gathered to talk about what the church of Jesus Christ might look like in the postmodern world of the twenty-first century. All the major denominations were represented. This was our first Summit, our invitation coming as a result of our Lifetree Café association with Group Publishing.

After an eventful and spiritually-fulfilling three days, the Summit culminated with a panel discussion on new forms of church. John White, co-founder and director of Luke 10 Ministries, a national network of house churches, tearfully shared what the Holy Spirit had said to him as he prepared his remarks for the Summit. John said that he realized that most of the Summit participants were there to learn new ways to "tweak" the existing church model, to find the magic bullet: the magic program, the magic worship style, the magic curriculum, the magic structure that would make the church of the twentieth century relevant in the twenty-first century. He was saddened by this revelation because he knew from twenty-five years of pastoral ministry how very difficult this "tweaking" work is, and how often it is ineffective and fruitless. In biblical terms, he realized how hopeless it is to continue to pour "new wine into old wineskins."[2]

Funny how a simple word like "tweaking" can stab you in the heart. We looked at each other. Like many of the people in the room that day, we had been stabbed in the heart. At that moment, we realized that we were among the 7+ million lay and clergy church leaders who were "almost DONE" with the institutional church. Thom Schultz, founder of Group Publishing and our host for the Summit, blogged a week later:

> At the conclusion of Group's Future of the Church summit, someone asked me, "What struck you most this week?" My answer surprised even me.
>
> The summit participants had explored several major trends that will affect the future of the church. We considered the implications of the growing population of Dones—those who have left the organized church, but not their faith. We explored non-traditional forms of church—house churches, dinner churches, even a surfer ministry. We experienced new and developing forms of corporate worship.
>
> But what struck me most wasn't even on the agenda. It came from the crowd. I was struck by the number of church leaders who quietly expressed their deep distress with their life in the church. After summit panelist and author Josh_ Packard described the Almost Dones—active church people who are ready to walk away—murmurs spread across the room. "He's describing me," a pastor said.[3]

We went directly from the Summit in Colorado to a major denominational meeting of pastors in Vancouver, Washington, and realized that we were scheduled to spend the next three days studying ways to "tweak" the existing model of church, when a whole new model was needed. We began the painful transition from "almost DONE" to "DONE."

Addicted? Really?

If addiction, as the *American Heritage Dictionary* states, is "the state of being enslaved to a habit or practice that is psychologically or physically habit-forming, such as narcotics, to such an extent that its cessation causes severe trauma," then the institutional church is "hooked."

If addiction is a habitual psychological dependence on a substance or practice beyond one's voluntary control, then the institutional church is hooked.

If addiction is a habitual or compulsive involvement in an activity, then both the institution and most local churches are addicted.

If addiction is a strong and harmful need to regularly have something (food, alcohol, narcotics, sexual intimacy) or do something (eat, drink, gamble, shop) then the institutional church and, in many cases, those attending are addicted.

Addicted? At first, that seemed a little harsh. We weren't enslaved to a habit-forming practice. We weren't psychologically dependent on a practice. We weren't habitually involved in an activity. Really?

In our attempts to be in relationship with God and lead others to follow Christ, we were addicted to all the practices and activities associated with the institutional church. The list was long: building management and maintenance; worship style, time, and place; office hours; and record keeping, reporting, and recording. None of these practices and activities enhanced our spiritual life or helped us model the life of a Jesus-follower. Yet we were enslaved to them and habitually focused on them.

Psychiatrist, spiritual counselor, and author Gerald May points out:

> The same processes that are responsible for addiction to alcohol and narcotics are also responsible for addiction to ideas, work, relationships, power, moods, fantasies, and an endless

variety of other things. We are all addicts in every sense of the word.

As a society we are addicted to work, performance, responsibility, intimacy, being liked, helping others, and an almost endless list of other behaviors.[4]

Sadly, we were beginning to realize that we were addicted to the trappings of church—the rules, rituals, and traditions of the institution.

Worship ≠ Following

Being DONE with church perhaps meant we were also done with religion, at least by the dictionary definitions of church and religion. We were done with institutionalized systems of attitudes, beliefs, and practices.

The church, the "Body of Christ," was more than ready to worship Jesus, but institutional survival was preventing the church from actually following Jesus through death, to resurrection and new life. As one reporter suggested to the Anglican Church in the United Kingdom, "It's time for the church to live into the life after death that it preaches." The institutional church is on life support in North America and Europe. It needs a "Living Will" so it can die with dignity and be raised by God in a fresh, new form.

Christian ≠ Jesus Follower

DONE with church, we were certainly not done with God, the God of the Bible. We were not finished with Jesus, with the Good News of the Gospel, or with the revolutionary things that Jesus said in the red letters of the Bible. Our desire to follow Jesus was stronger than ever.

We were DONE with the institutional church and its metrics. We were DONE with counting people in the pews and dollars in the plate, at the expense of teaching discipleship through sacrifice, risk-taking, and accountability. We were done with institutionalized religion and its emphasis on denomination (read "tribe"). We were DONE with the competition and comparison among clergy and congregants. The more we thought and prayed about it, the more certain we became that God and Jesus are DONES as well. We discovered that we didn't have to belong to a particular church or denomination to follow Jesus. We didn't even have to be Christian to follow Jesus. But we're getting ahead of ourselves.

Step 1

The first step toward overcoming an addiction is to admit, or confess, that we are addicted, and that we are powerless to control our addiction!

Hi, I'm Gerri! Hi, I'm Stan! We're churchaholics. We can't change the church, and we can't restore our own spirituality.

The name of this step is SURRENDER.

I realize that I don't have what it takes. I can will it, but I can't *do* it. I decide to do good, but I don't *really* do it; I decide not to do bad, but then I do it anyway. My decisions, such as they are, don't result in actions. Something has gone wrong deep within me and it gets the better of me every time (Romans 7:18–20, The Message).

Something to Think About...

Rituals, rules, and traditions provide an element of comfort and certainty in our lives and in our faith communities. These are social actions whereby certain activities are performed at set times and places and have a set order. When they just happen without focus or intent they become meaningless.

Many times we just "show up" because we "should," without intent, focus, or engagement. We "go through the motions" but are internally detached from any meaningful connection to God or others.

- *In your faith community, i.e., church, what practices do you participate in that draw you closer to God?*
- *Which rituals, rules, and traditions are just "what we do" in a worship service and do not help you connect to God?*
- *Which ones could you give up?*

Endnotes

[1] Alcoholics Anonymous World Services. *Big Book of Alcoholics Anonymous*, 4th Edition, 2001, page 59.

[2] John White, *Why I broke down in tears at "The Future of the Church Summit,"* www.lk10.com/blog, October 25, 2015.

[3] Thom Schultz, *The Pending Exit of the Clergy*, Holy Soup.com, November 4, 2015.

[4] Gerald G. May, MD, *Addiction and Grace: Love and Spirituality in the Healing of Addictions*, HarperCollins Publishers, 1988, pages 3–4 and 9.

Step 2

God Can

We came to believe that God could transform
the church and restore our spirituality.

When we confess that we can't overcome our addiction to the rules, rituals, and traditions of the institutional church and restore our own spirituality, we've taken the first step. Remember, step 1 is "surrender." Step 1 is about letting go of our pride and self-will. Step 2 is about letting go of preconceived notions about church and spirituality and trusting God to transform the church and change us.

DONES are folks who have given up on the institutional church and institutionalized religion but not on God. Most DONES have been hurt by the institutional church, and hurt badly. Someone said, "Religion is lived by people who are afraid of hell. Spirituality is lived by people who have been through hell." Our spirituality needs to be restored. Only God can do that.

Betrayed and Discouraged

We would like to shun the pain and despair that surrender can bring. We would like to deny that we have hit "rock bottom" and we want to quickly jump to a "new normal." We don't want to sit in the darkness, experience the losses, and suffer the sorrow and broken-heartedness that are part of surrender. This is a lie. This is to deny life's experiences.

Gerri's story continues ...

> Being DONE with the institutional church left a huge void in my life. I no longer had others to please, conform to, entertain, or convince. Most of those in our congregation were not interested in following Jesus in the way that Jesus had instructed in those red letters in the Bible. I had been a member of this church for 25 years. Some of these people were long time friends of mine.
>
> Once I moved toward seminary and leadership, the relationship changed. I no longer felt accepted or supported, though I was told that that was not so.
>
> Actions speak louder than words. As the Gospel compelled us to speak up and out for Jesus and his way of life, when it challenged us to speak words of justice and truth, when we represented a ministry centered on Jesus, when we called others to take up their cross and follow Jesus, when we called for change, we became very unpopular. The more that the status quo was challenged through preaching and teaching, the more the ruling class of the institution was challenged by new wine that called for new wineskins, the more resistance we met.
>
> These friends and "members" of the institutional church began to fall away. "Not here, not now. It's not who we are."
>
> It was too much to ask. Jesus asked too much.

The Gospel of John says in chapter 15:18–19, (NLT, Jesus-Centered Bible) "If the world hates you, remember that it hated me first. The world would love you as one of its own if you belonged to it, but you are no longer part of the world. I chose you to come out of the world, so it hates you." Betrayal, hurt, deep sadness, it all enveloped me.

And I, I thought that I could read a Psalm of lament once or twice, say a prayer and move on to what Jesus was calling me to do; to lead those that are interested in actually following Jesus, no matter what.

Like the rest of the culture, hurt and negativity is not where I wanted to spend any time. I am not a victim. "Get over it and move on" was my mantra.

We Came to Believe …

We finally came to believe that God is not a part of the darkness but is present in the darkness with us. When we put our hope in God, the One who says, "Fear not," we find the darkness gets transformed to light and new life.

When the going gets tough and we've exhausted all of our own resources, when most of our friends have deserted us, when we finally acknowledge that we can't change the world, or even the church, that's when we typically turn to God. Even Jesus had days like that.

When Jesus's teaching became difficult and offended people, many of his followers turned away. He turned to his closest friends and followers and asked, "Do you also wish to go away?" Simon Peter answered him, "Lord, to whom can we go? You have the words of eternal life. We have come to believe and know that you are the Holy One of God" (John 6:66–69, New Revised Standard Version).

We came to believe and know that we can't transform the world or even ourselves, that only God can.

Lookin' for God in All the Wrong Places

We DONES need to remind ourselves that God works in mysterious ways, that God's ways are not our ways, that God works on God's schedule, and that God has a plan. We need to remind ourselves that God never fails and that God will never fail us.

Spiritual growth cannot be packaged, programmed or taught. It is a "giving up" more than an acquisition. We had read the most current, popular "Christian" books, written by contemporary, forward-thinking theologians and Christian authors. We had listened to and sung the newest "Christian" music, participated in popular spiritual formation gatherings and attended multiple Bible studies. We felt no closer to God. We were still trying to be in control. We were still making a plan, scheduling God's arrival. Apparently, God was unaware of our schedule!

Transformation does not come by way of information or education. Transformation is God's doing. When we began realize that God does not provide answers and that God is the answer, our transformation began. We had to begin the hard work of walking through the valley of the shadow of death and doubt. There are many ways to do that. There is no magic formula.

Transformation comes through silence, prayer, simple words, music, art, writing poetry, or other means of emptying the mind. This is the action that God requires. When we focused less on "following the rules" and focused more on spending time just being the humans that God created us to be, we found the freedom to love and serve others, ALL others.

When the burden of trying to please others was lessened and we were free to focus on following Jesus and loving God our relationships became deeper. This is the joy of God's transforming power!

Gerald May says that he is convinced that all human beings have an inborn desire for God, that this desire is our deepest longing and is what gives us meaning.[1] In order to fulfill that desire for God, we must have a relationship with God. We must transfer our faith and hope from the church and religion, to faith and hope in God. Faith is about having an open mind, about allowing God to show us new and amazing ways to think and live. Hope is about having a humble heart, open to the unlimited and unconditional love that God wants to pour into us.

Faith and hope go hand in hand. The author of Hebrews says that, "Faith shows the reality of what we hope for; it is the evidence of things we cannot see" (Hebrews 11:1, NLT, Jesus-Centered Bible).

Only God can! Say it with us! Say it out loud! Make it your breath prayer, "Only God can!" Don't skip this step. Even if your first reaction is, "Well, duh!" Say it until you come to believe it and know it at your very core, "Only God can!"

Step 2

Hi, I'm Gerri! Hi, I'm Stan! We're churchaholics. We have come to believe and know that God can transform the church and restore our spirituality.

The name of this step is HOPE.

We pray that God, the source of hope will fill you completely with joy and peace because you trust in him (Romans 15:13, NLT, Jesus-Centered Bible).

Something to Think About ...

Spiritual growth cannot be packaged, programmed, or taught. Transformation does not come by way of information or education; it is God's doing. Staying connected to God through faith and hope opens the way for God's transforming power.

Brokenness or broken heartedness is usually due to some kind of loss, voluntary or not.

- *When have you experienced brokenness or broken heartedness due to loss?*
- *How did you react? Did you sit with the loss or quickly move to something else in order to "get over it"? What was the result?*
- *If we all have an inborn desire for God, where and how do you seek God? What brings you closer to hearing God speak in your life?*

Endnote

1. Gerald G. May, MD. *Addiction and Grace: Love and Spirituality in the Healing of Addictions*, HarperCollins Publishers, 1988, page 8.

Step 3

Let God

*We made a decision to turn the church and our
spirituality over to the care of God.*

Step 1 is about letting go of our pride and self-will. Step 2 is about letting go of preconceived notions about church and spirituality. We've let go of a lot of "stuff," now what?

Nature abhors a vacuum. Giving up the rules, rituals, and traditions of the institutional church will certainly create emptiness, a vacuum in our lives. The busyness of "church life" will be absent. The routine of obeying the rules, observing the rituals, and honoring the traditions will be gone. Will we begin to feel the pain of missing that routine? What will replace those practices? What will keep us from backsliding into the easier, non-fulfilling practices of "doing church" or doing nothing?

Jesus says that when one demon leaves and finds nowhere to rest, it returns to a clean house with seven of its friends. The host is worse off than ever before! (Luke 12:23–24).

Addicted to "Warm and Fuzzy"

We were trapped by the need for the spiritual hit that the institutional church provided by means of a Sunday morning worship service. Sunday is the day, mid-morning is the time. Attend, sing, pray, listen, and then check the box marked "your spiritual life" and be finished for the week, the month, or the season. At times, the experience was pleasurable; the music or liturgy produced a warm fuzzy "spiritual high," but this was emotion, and perhaps the emotion was what we were addicted to.

Our bodies, minds, and spirits were dominated by the rules, rituals, and traditions of the church. We were living in the land of "should"—tit for tat. I'll follow the rules and God will give me all I want/need. Rick Lawrence says that hearts crave more than the *shoulded* relationship with Jesus that the religious culture force feeds us, that "shoulding motivation is always pushing us toward religious imperatives—the determined do's and don'ts of what passes for our spiritual life … Following should-laws offers a twisted comfort but it is short lived."[1]

We didn't realize that deep loss and amazing gifts are held in a powerful tension: sadness and joy, loss and hope.

Our desiring and longing for spirituality must be deepened and broadened. Richard Rohr says that we have three places that need to be opened within us in order for this deepening of spirituality to take place: "Our opinionated head, our closed-down heart and our defensive and defended body."[2]

Speaking of "our opinionated head," step 3 moves us to action. A decision is made in your head. We must be honest about our beliefs and spiritual life if we are to grow spiritually. Decisions require action. We made a decision; it was not made for us. We moved from "I can't" to "God can" to "Let God" and that decision leads us out of bondage into freedom. We acknowledge and embrace our dependence on God.

Steps 1 and 2 are about reflection and introspection, but step 3 moves us forward from thinking to action, from following our own will to conforming to God's will. In step 3, we need to create a plan for letting God into our lives, really in, as in … "all in!"

We've been in religious circles all our lives and usually find very few who actually turn their lives over to God. Our willfulness runs rampant among clergy and laity, regardless of rank or standing. Renouncing ourselves and radically surrendering our will to the One we trust more than ourselves is indeed an action item! There is real freedom in authentic spiritual surrender. Paradoxically, a broken heart often precedes this "letting go and let God" step.

A decision requires action. Action reduces fear. When fear is reduced, hope and faith blossom.

If God Is Your Co-Pilot, Switch Seats!

The Alcoholics Anonymous *Big Book* provides this analogy of the first three steps:[3]

> Being convinced, *we were at Step Three*, which is that we decided to turn our will and our life over to God. Just what do we mean by that, and just what do we do?
>
> The first requirement is that we be convinced that any life run on self-will can hardly be a success. Each person is like an actor who wants to run the whole show; is forever trying to arrange the lights, the ballet, the scenery and the rest of the players in his own way. If the arrangements would only stay put, if only people would do as he or she wished, the show would be great. Everyone would be pleased. Life would be wonderful.

Sounds a lot like a denominational leader meeting, or a local church worship team meeting, or finding the perfect curriculum or program, doesn't it? If we can just say and do the next "right" thing, people will flock to our churches and become followers of Jesus. More from the *Big Book*:

> What usually happens? The show doesn't come off very well. He or she begins to think that life isn't fair. He or she decides to work even harder. Still the play isn't good enough.

This recurring drama is being played out time and time again. People are drawn to God or Jesus and they end up in a church. They start to become comfortable with the rules, rituals, and traditions (they get their weekly spirituality "fix") and become centered on the institution that provides the fix. No wonder Jesus looked out over Jerusalem and the Temple and cried (Luke 19:41–44). How easy it is for us to get off-center.

> This is the how and why of it. First of all, we had to quit playing God. It didn't work. Next, we decided that hereafter in this drama of life, God was going to be our Director.

Surrender to God, have hope in God, take action to let God direct your life.

Keep on Keepin' On

The twelve steps are not a checklist; they are a process. Even as we work the steps, we are constantly going back to step 1, to surrender our pride and self-will all over again. With God's help, every positive step is a step closer to unconditional surrender.

Richard Rohr adds, "The surrender of faith does not happen in one moment but is an extended journey, a trust walk, a gradual letting go, unlearning and handing over. No one does it on the first or even second try."

Step 3

Hi, I'm Gerri! Hi, I'm Stan! We're churchaholics.
We made a decision to turn the church and our
spirituality over to the care of God.

The name of this step is FAITH.

Be still, be calm, see and understand I am the True God (Psalm 46:10, The Voice).

Something to Think About ...

A decision demands action. If we have decided to "let God," then we need to change some things in our lives so that God can work.

- *We are addicted to many comfortable self-serving images of faith. Which ones are you addicted to? Music style, prayer preferences, worship time, day, format?*
- *How do the "shoulds" affect your behavior when it comes to your spiritual life, i.e., "I should cover my tattoo when I go to church"? Do you think that God really cares if you have a tattoo?*
- *How would it feel to give up those preferences and trust God to challenge and lead you to follow Jesus rather than just observing the "shoulds" when it comes to rules, rituals and traditions?*

Endnotes

1. Rick Lawrence. *The Jesus-Centered Life*, Group Publishing, Loveland CO, 2016, page 51.
2. Richard Rohr. *Breathing Under Water: Spirituality and the Twelve Steps*, St. Anthony Messenger Press, 2011 (Kindle).
3. Alcoholics Anonymous World Services. *Big Book of Alcoholics Anonymous*, 4th Edition, 2001, pages 60–62.

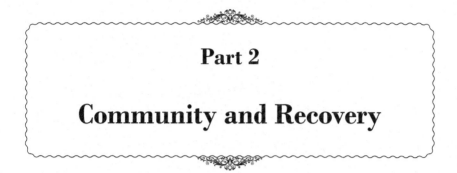

Part 2

Community and Recovery

Life in community is no less than a necessity for us—
it is an inescapable "must"
that determines everything we do and think.

—Eberhard Arnold
Why We Live in Community

Step 4

Look Within

We made a searching and fearless spiritual inventory of ourselves.

The purpose of step 4 is to determine the causes and conditions of our addiction to the institutions of church and religion and to assess where we are spiritually.

The purpose of taking a personal inventory of our spiritual life is to rid ourselves of the traps and burdens that control us and to free ourselves from living in old useless patterns. The complaining and resentment that lead to reliving the circumstances that brought us to this place are of no value. It was time to move forward, one baby step at a time. During this introspective inventory, we will disclose the damaged goods, and then get rid of them, as well as the excess stuff we carry around in our heads and our hearts. Our goal is to be finished with the past, not to cling to it. The old saying is, "Don't look back unless you intend to go that way."

We wanted to skip this step. We wanted to just put this behind us and get on with life. It would be easier, or so we thought. It would also be far less genuine. We needed to struggle through the inventory and engage in recovery with courage and stamina ... no matter what!

The *Big Book* of Alcoholics Anonymous provides this business analogy for conducting an honest and thorough inventory:

A business which takes no regular inventory usually goes broke. Taking a commercial inventory is a fact-finding and a fact-facing process. It is an effort to discover the truth about the stock-in-trade. One object is to disclose damaged or unsalable goods, to get rid of them promptly and without regret.

We accomplished our personal spiritual inventory by asking a series of questions and answering them honestly.

Going to Church or Being the Church

We determined that the cause of our addiction to the institutional church was *going to church*. So we had to ask, "Why did we go to church?" The answers varied:

We grew up going to church. (social)

That's what good people did. (social)

So others would think that we were good people. (social)

We *should* go to church. (social)

In order to get into heaven. (personal)

So God would like us. (personal)

We went to church for a variety of reasons, some valid and some not so much. A related question surfaced during the inventory: *"What was the purpose of attending and being a member of a church?"* Those answers varied also:

To belong somewhere. (social)

To meet our own expectations for being a good person. (personal)

To meet the expectations of others. (social)

For entertainment. (personal)

To be with the right people. (social)

To be seen. (social)

Damn! We were going to church and becoming members to serve ourselves and meet social expectations.

"What did we expect this church affiliation to provide for us?"

On our best days, we expected it to provide a connection with God by way of answers to our many questions.

Among them are the following:

What am I here for? What is my purpose in life? What is my mission? What am I supposed to *do*? Where is the checklist?

Problem! There was indeed a checklist and it wasn't God's checklist. It was a checklist based on the rules, rituals, and traditions of the institutional church.

The checklist included but was not limited to

- Serve … on committees.
- Give … to the budget.
- Worship … weekly, if convenient and comfortable. But worship who, or what?
- Pray … for what you want for yourself and others. But pray to whom?

We realized that:

- Serving on committees did not necessarily serve the hungry, thirsty, homeless, sick, and imprisoned in our community (Matthew 25:31–45).
- Giving to the church budget was not the same as giving joyfully and sacrificially to God's work before we paid the bills (Deuteronomy 26:1–11, Malachi 3:8–10, Luke 21:1–4, Acts 2:42–46).
- Worship had become more about the building, the music, the rituals, the pastors, the furniture, and the decorations, than it was about connecting with God and growing in the Spirit. People were coming to "feel good" and be entertained, not to be challenged and encouraged

on the road of discipleship (2 Kings 18:3–6, Hosea 6:6, Matthew 19:3).

- Praying to the Santa Claus god that provided everything we wanted was not working. We were reciting the Lord's Prayer without hearing it. If we prayed "Not my will, but Thy will be done," we didn't really mean it (Matthew 6:5–13, Matthew 26:39).

After fifty-plus years, this was obviously not working. Even after we became pastors, those whom culture expects to be "especially close to God," our connection to God remained tenuous, and felt as thin as the veneer on cheap furniture.

Why didn't this work?

Pogo said, "We have seen the enemy, and it is us."

We were no closer to God because somewhere along the way we had missed the part where our spirituality is our responsibility, not something we can purchase in a store called "church."

Yes, the church has missed the mark. The culture has invaded what was "sacred space." But we, the people, have allowed this to happen.

When the church became an institution, a ward of the state, a religious icon, serving the culture instead of transforming it, we, the people, stood silently by and allowed the movement of the Holy Spirit to become just another activity in our busy lives.

During the "if you build it, they will come" phase of church in the United States and Western Europe, when the church was the culturally-correct place to be, all was well. When the culture shifted and other forms of entertainment and "belonging" became available, the church was in trouble.

We silently and obediently stood by and let the professional clergy and the institution do the work of being church, and we became mere consumers in the spirituality marketplace. The church was just another place to go … if we had time.

Back to the Future

Philosopher George Santayana said, "Those who cannot remember the past are condemned to repeat it." Another way to say that is: If you want a new idea, read an old book. Surely this is not the first time that God's people have struggled with institutional church and institutionalized religion. Let's "go back to the future"… from the prophet Amos, chapter 5, verses 21–24, in The Message, God is speaking:

> "I can't stand your religious meetings.
>   I'm fed up with your conferences and conventions.
> I want nothing to do with your religion projects,
>   your pretentious slogans and goals.
> I'm sick of your fund-raising schemes,
>   your public relations and image making.
> I've had all I can take of your noisy ego-music.
>   When was the last time you sang to *me?*
> Do you know what I want?
>   I want justice—oceans of it.
> I want fairness—rivers of it.
>   That's what I want. That's *all* I want."

Okay, time to take a look within ourselves. The institutional church and its leaders may be hung up on the survival of the institution and their careers but what about us? What about my own "religious life?"

The prophet Micah had this to say about what God wants from us (Micah 6:6–8, MSG):

"How can I stand up before GOD
  and show proper respect to the high God?
Should I bring an armload of offerings
  topped off with yearling calves?
Would GOD be impressed with thousands of rams,
  with buckets and barrels of olive oil?
Would GOD be moved if I sacrificed my firstborn child,
  my precious baby, to cancel my sin?
    But GOD's already made it plain how to live, what to do,
  what GOD is looking for in men and women.
It's quite simple: Do what is fair and just to your neighbor,
  be compassionate and loyal in your love,
And don't take yourself too seriously—
  take God seriously."

This is what God wants: love, justice, humility. If that's what God wants, how were we doing? Did we believe in God, or did we believe God? We found our lives fell short.

We worked hard each week to plan a meaningful worship service. We tried hard to make worship worshipful. We also backed off at times when we knew that the message would make some uncomfortable. We appeased the congregation and over indulged them in "feel good" conversations instead of preaching what it would look like to actually follow Jesus. Hard-wired by the institution of church, part of our job was to keep people coming in to fill the pews and collection plates. We needed to meet the target numbers and keep the doors open.

Again, the question: How was what we were doing day to day to day meeting God's expectations? Did our worship services inspire others to love, do justice, and act with humility; or were they mere ritual, pageantry, and performance? Did rule, ritual, and tradition shape them, or were they deep expressions of sacrifice, brokenness, and trust in God? Were they self-serving or life changing? Did we call the shots in order to please others, or was

God in control? Was the Gospel being presented as the Gospel, no matter what?

Unless each ministry we led and participated in was focused on making disciples for the transformation of the world, we were not doing as God commanded. Doing for the purpose of doing does not fulfill us. A program is just a program unless it leads others to Christ. It is no wonder that our lives were filled with anxiety and exhaustion ... this path did not lead toward God, it led nowhere. The addiction needed to end. Our spirits were dying.

"So here's what I want you to do, *God* helping you: Take your everyday, ordinary life—your sleeping, eating, going-to-work, and walking-around life—and place it before God as an offering. Embracing what God does for you is the best thing you can do for God. Don't become so well-adjusted to your culture that you fit into it without even thinking. Instead, fix your attention on God. You'll be changed from the inside out. Readily recognize what God wants from you, and quickly respond to it. Unlike the culture around you, always dragging you down to its level of immaturity, God brings the best out of you, develops well-formed maturity in you" (Romans 12:1–2 MSG).

We discovered that individuals and movements are changed from the inside out while institutions are changed from the outside in. Okay then, seemed simple enough: Stop doing what we had been doing and start doing what God wants us to do. Simple? Yes. Easy? No.

Step 4

Hi, I'm Gerri! Hi, I'm Stan! We're churchaholics. We made a searching and fearless spiritual inventory of ourselves.

The name of this step is HONESTY.

Step 4 is about creating a good and trustworthy lamp inside of us that reflects and reveals what is really there, knowing that "anything exposed to the light will itself become light" (Ephesians 5:14).

—Richard Rohr, *Breathing Under Water*

Something to Think About ...

- *Take your own spiritual inventory. Answer honestly.*
- *Why do you, or did you, go to church? What is/was its purpose in your life?*
- *What do you expect from a church affiliation?*
- *Do, or did you, expect that attending a church will or would bring you into a relationship with God?*
- *What would it look like to take responsibility for your own spiritual growth?*

Admit Wrongs

We admitted to God, to ourselves, and to another human being the exact nature of our failures.

In step 4, we took a fearless inventory of our spiritual lives. Writing the inventory is helpful, essential even, but it is not the end. We all tend to live secretly, not wanting others to know our shortcomings and failures. A secret remains a secret until it is shared. When we talk through our personal inventory with another person, someone we trust, it creates accountability and responsibility. When we ask and receive forgiveness the result is freedom! Step 5 is the key to freedom.

The Dreaded Hall Closet

In Robert Boyd Munger's classic story about a man who turns his heart into Christ's home, room by room, there's one last secret "room" that must be opened and shared, The Hall Closet:

> There's one more matter of crucial con-
> sequence I would like to share with you. One
> day I found him *[Christ]* waiting for me at the
> front door. An arresting look was in his eye. As I

entered, he said to me, "There's a peculiar odor in the house. Something must be dead around here. It's upstairs. I think it is in the hall closet."

As soon as he said this I knew what he was talking about. Indeed there was a small closet up there on the hall landing, just a few feet square. In that closet behind lock and key I had one or two little personal things I did not want anybody to know about. Certainly I did not want Christ to see them. They were dead and rotting things left over from the old life—not wicked, but not right and good to have in a Christian life. Yet I loved them. I wanted them so much for myself I was really afraid to admit they were there. Reluctantly I went up the stairs with him and as we mounted, the odor became stronger and stronger. He pointed at the door and said, "It's in there! Some dead thing!"

It made me angry! That's the only way I can put it. I had given him access to the study, the dining room, the living room, the workroom, the rec room, the bedroom, the family room, the kitchen—and now he was asking me about a little two-by-four closet. I said to myself, "This is too much! I am not going to give him the key."

"Well," he responded, reading my thoughts, "if you think I am going to stay up here on the second floor with this smell, you are mistaken. I will take my bed out to the back porch or somewhere else. I'm certainly not going to stay around that." And I saw him start down the stairs.

When you have come to know and love Jesus Christ, one of the worst things that can happen is to sense him withdrawing his face and fellowship. I had to give in. "I'll give you the key," I said sadly, "but you'll have to open the closet and clean it out. I haven't the strength to do it."

"I know," he said. "I know you haven't. Just give me the key. Just authorize me to handle that closet and I will." So with trembling fingers, I passed the key over to him. He took it from my hand, walked over to the door, opened it, entered it, took out the putrefying stuff that was rotting there and threw it away. Then he cleansed the closet, painted it and fixed it up all in a moment's time. Immediately a fresh, fragrant breeze swept through the house. The whole atmosphere changed. What release and victory to have that dead thing out of my life! No matter what sin or what pain there might be in my past, Jesus is ready to forgive, to heal and to make whole.[1]

We all have "hall closets" filled with secrets. Once our spiritual inventory identifies those secrets, it's time to share.

The Apostle Paul understood that just doing the inventory is not enough. We need to admit our wrongs to God, to ourselves, and to someone we trust with our most embarrassing secrets.

But I need something *more!* For if I know the law but still can't keep it, and if the power of sin within me keeps sabotaging my best intentions, I obviously need help! I realize that I don't have what it takes. I can will it, but I can't *do* it. I decide to do good, but I don't *really* do it; I decide not to do bad, but then I do it anyway. My decisions, such as they are, don't result in actions. Something has gone wrong deep within me and gets the better of me every time.

It happens so regularly that it's predictable. The moment I decide to do good, sin is there to trip me up. I truly delight in God's commands, but it's pretty obvious that not all of me joins in that delight. Parts of me covertly rebel, and just when I least expect it, they take charge.

I've tried everything and nothing helps. I'm at the end of my rope. Is there no one who can do anything for me? Isn't that the real question? (Romans 7:17–24, MSG)

All Aboard!

This step calls for complete honesty. Find someone with whom you can be completely honest. This needs to be someone that you can be honest with about spiritual and emotional issues. You will also need to trust them with family and financial details. All these areas of life are crucial to spiritual well-being. Spirit is not confined to one corner of our life. It encompasses all of life. For an unbiased, completely neutral listening ear, it will be necessary to find someone other than a family member to have this conversation with.

We needed to be honest about where we had been: addicted to rules, regulations, and traditions and about what we needed to become: true followers of Jesus. We needed to be able to articulate what we would be willing to give up, in order to be true to our call. We needed to trust each other and not hold back. Honest feedback was a requirement. At times, this was difficult. However, we agreed to keep an open mind, pass no judgment, and offer compassion and understanding.

Believing that God speaks and acts through others, we agreed to try to be the hands, feet, and voice of Christ for one another. We looked together at who we were and what we were doing. It looked like pretense and playing church. We could and needed to do better. We wanted to do what Jesus commanded, no matter what.

This time of accountability and confession is like a stop at the train station. We unloaded our junk. We let go of our anger, shame, and regret and grabbed a new ticket.

> This train is bound for glory, this train
> This train is bound for glory, this train
> This train is bound for glory
> Don't carry nothing but the righteous and the holy
> This train is bound for glory, this train[2]

We cleaned out the cobwebs of the past and took a deep breath; we needed to relax and enjoy the ride and to soak in the scenery of God's unconditional love. We were headed to freedom. This new freedom was a place to be ourselves, to be all that God created us to be, to dream new dreams and allow passion once again to fuel our journey. All aboard!

Free to Surrender

The key to our freedom is to remain responsible for the choices we make in response to that freedom. Remember that our addiction cannot be defeated by our own willpower, nor can we "opt out" and turn everything over to divine will. We don't just get to say, "Here's my junk, here's all my bad stuff, God!" and walk away. We can only trust God when we act responsibly.

Gerald May says, "Responsible human freedom thus becomes authentic spiritual surrender, and authentic spiritual surrender is nothing other than responsible human freedom."[3]

Sharing our spiritual inventory with God is responsible. Sharing our inventory with another person makes us accountable.

Step 5

Hi, I'm Gerri! Hi, I'm Stan! We're churchaholics.
We admitted to God, to ourselves, and to another
human being the exact nature of our failures.

The name of this step is TRUST.

Make this your common practice: Confess your sins to each other and pray for each other so that you can live together whole and healed. The prayer of a person living right with God is something powerful to be reckoned with (James 5:16–17, MSG).

Something to Think About ...

No matter how hard we try, on our own we can't change our addictive behavior. We can't just dump all the junk, all the bad stuff, in our lives on God and walk away. We can trust God to help us change when we act responsibly.

- *Name one secret that you keep in your "hall closet."*
- *Is there another person that you can trust with that secret?*
- *Are you willing to share that secret with God and another in order to leave it in the past and grab a ticket to the future?*

Endnotes

[1.] Robert Boyd Munger. *My Heart ~ Christ's Home*, 2nd Edition, InterVarsity Press, Downers Grove IL, 1992, pages 37–40.
[2.] Woody Guthrie. *This Train*, adapted from African American Folk song.
[3.] Gerald G. May, MD. *Addiction and Grace: Love and Spirituality in the Healing of Addictions*, HarperCollins Publishers, 1988, page 139.

Ready Self for Change

We were entirely ready and willing to have God remove our defects of character and failures.

This step sounds like a "no-brainer" and we were tempted to push right through to the next step. Obviously, we were ready to have God remove our defects of character and failures. Who wouldn't be? Not so fast! Maybe we're not as ready and willing as we think!

Is There Anyone Else up There?

A man named Jack was walking along a steep cliff one day when he accidentally got too close to the edge and fell. On the way down he grabbed a branch, which temporarily stopped his fall. He looked down and to his horror saw that the drop below him was more than 500 feet, and he knew he couldn't hang on to the branch forever.

So Jack began yelling for help, hoping that someone passing by would hear and lower a rope or do something.

"Help! Help! Is anyone up there? Help!" Jack yelled. But no one heard him. He was about to give up when he heard a voice, "Jack, Jack. Can you hear me?"

"Yes, yes! I can hear you. I'm down here!"

"I can see you, Jack. Are you all right?"

"No! Yes! But, who are you and where are you?"

"I am the Lord, Jack. I'm everywhere."

"The Lord? You mean GOD?"

"That's me."

"Oh, God, please help me! I promise that if You get me down from here, I'll really be a good person. I'll go to church every Sunday and serve you for the rest of my life."

"Easy on the promises, Jack. Now, here's what I want you to do. Listen carefully."

"I'll do anything, Lord. Just tell me."

"Okay. Let go of the branch."

"What?"

"I said, let go of the branch. Trust me. Let go."

There was a long silence.

Finally, Jack yelled, "Help! Help! Help! Is there anyone else up there?"[1]

Do You Wanna Be Well?

Soon another Feast came around and Jesus was back in Jerusalem. Near the Sheep Gate in Jerusalem there was a pool, in Hebrew called *Bethesda*, with five alcoves. Hundreds of sick people—blind, crippled, paralyzed—were in these alcoves. One man had been an invalid there for thirty-eight years. When Jesus saw him stretched out by the pool and knew how long he had been there, he said, "Do you want to get well?"

The sick man said, "Sir, when the water is stirred, I don't have anybody to put me in the pool. By the time I get there, somebody else is already in."

Jesus said, "Get up, take your bedroll, start walking." The man was healed on the spot. He picked up his bedroll and walked off. (John 5:1–9, MSG)

William Barclay, world-renowned New Testament scholar, helps us understand this strange story: "Beneath the pool was a subterranean stream which every now and again bubbled up and disturbed the waters. The belief was that the disturbance was caused by an angel, and that the first person to get into the pool after the troubling *(stirring)* of the water would be healed from any illness from which he or she was suffering."[2]

Barclay goes on to cite four things we should learn from this miraculous healing:

1. Jesus began by asking the man if he wanted to be cured. The man had waited for thirty-eight years … In his heart of hearts the man might be well content to remain an invalid … He might have grown accustomed to his disability … But his response was immediate … He wanted to be healed. The first essential to receiving the power of Jesus is to have intense desire for it. Jesus says: 'Do you really want to be changed?' If in our inmost hearts we are well content to stay as we are, there can be no change for us.

In order to really want to change we must find ourselves at the end of our rope. We need to be desperate for a new way of life.

God then becomes the knot at the end of our rope, the knot that we hold on to. We were at the end of our rope with the institutional church.

Until that happens, we just remain scared and lazy. We once saw a sign that read, "God, I want to change, but I am too scared and lazy." Sadly, that sums it up for many of us stuck in the routine and comfort of rule, ritual, and tradition. Surrender, again and again, is the fuel that ignites the fuse of change.

2. Jesus went on to tell the man to get up ... The power of God never dispenses with human effort. Nothing is truer than we must realize our own helplessness; but in a very real sense it is true that miracles happen when our will and God's power co-operate to make them possible.

"Analysis paralysis" ... we felt God nudging us to action. You've probably felt it too. And then you think about it. And ponder it. And weigh the pros and cons. And make excuses. Was that really God? Maybe it was just me. When God whispers in your ear, it will most often be inconvenient and a bit uncomfortable. But when you comply ... voila! The joy and satisfaction you receive when you cooperate with God's Spirit are remarkable. God has a plan for us. We realized that alone we could do nothing. But with God's power, through us, anything in God's plan was possible.

3. In effect, Jesus was commanding the man to attempt the impossible ... The man might well have said with a kind of injured resentment that for thirty-eight years his bed had been carrying him and there was not much sense in telling him to carry it. But he made the effort along with Christ— and the thing was done.

We have noticed that when we move ahead, paying attention to God's direction, trusting the Spirit to guide us, we make progress.

When we move with God, doors open. The path may not be easy, but it is simple.

4.   Here is the road to achievement. There are so many things in this world which defeat us. *When we have intensity of desire and determination to make the effort, hopeless though it may seem, the power of Christ gets its opportunity, and with him we can conquer things that for a long time have conquered us* [emphasis added].[3]

Intentional engagement with the community, following Jesus's two rules (love God and love others), paying attention to the opportunities to be of service and not becoming distracted by the culture that says, "Me first!" and focusing on living like Jesus lived, no matter what. That is the road to recovery and spiritual wellness.

Trust and Obey, for There's No Other Way …

Jack, our cliff-hanging hero, was ready to be saved, but not ready to trust God. Jack was also willing to let God save him, but was unwilling to let go of the branch that was keeping him attached to his old way of life. The man by the well in Jerusalem was ready to trust God and willing to attempt the impossible in order to be healed … in order to overcome his addiction to the rules, rituals, and traditions of his time.

Like Jack, we are more than ready to let God fix us, but only on our terms. We are ready and willing to believe in God, but we are often unwilling to let go and believe that God will catch us. We call it the "ignorance and arrogance" factor. We are arrogant enough to think we know what is best for us; but we are, in reality, largely ignorant of what we need.

God is always ready and willing to remove our character defects and failures … but there's a catch. Believing God and following Jesus is a participatory sport, not a spectator sport. There's that "Do you believe God, or just believe in God?" question again! Jesus has more than enough fans. What he needs are followers. Believing God and following Jesus is a team sport, not an individual sport. In order to beat our addictions we need to team up with God and with a community.

In step 4, we did a searching and fearless spiritual inventory. In step 5, we shared that inventory with someone in our community that we trusted completely, a friend who would hold us accountable while withholding judgment. In step 6, we must go deep, to our "inmost heart," to make sure that we are ready and willing to let God change us.

We must truthfully answer "yes" to these questions:

Are we really ready to change?

Are we willing to do whatever God tells us to do?

We must not move on to step 7 until we can. Don't skip or move too quickly through this step!

Step 6

Hi, I'm Gerri! Hi, I'm Stan! We're churchaholics.
We were entirely ready and willing to have God
remove our defects of character and failures.

The name of this step is WILLINGNESS.

Do you wanna be well, really wanna be well?
Are you willing to take up your mat and help yourself?
Do you wanna be free, really wanna be free?
If you wanna be healed and whole, you gotta wanna be well.
—Gaither Vocal Band, *Do You Wanna Be Well*
Song lyric based on John 5:1–9

Something to Think About ...

Great things seldom come from comfort zones. We can become victims of our comfort and convenience. God calls us to more.

- *If the phrase "scared and lazy" applies to you, what can you do to move ahead?*
- *How do you work your way out of the "analysis paralysis" that prevents you from moving forward?*

Endnotes

1. *The World's Greatest Collection of Church Jokes*, Compiled and Edited by Paul M. Miller, Barbour Publishing, Uhrichsville OH, 2003 pages 229–231.
2. William Barclay, *The New Daily Study Bible, The Gospel of John, Volume One*, Westminster John Knox Press, Louisville KY, 2001, page 209.
3. Ibid, page 210.

Seek God's Help

*We humbly asked God to remove our
shortcomings and renew our spirits.*

Step 7 is an action step. We prepared our spiritual inventories, we shared them honestly with one another, and then we readied ourselves to accept God's help and guidance. It's time to humbly pray for God to change us, to ask God to clean out the bad stuff and backfill with the Holy Spirit.

That's Not What I Asked For!

When the people following Jesus noticed how much strength and energy he got from prayer, they asked for instructions so they could get what he got from God. But Jesus seems to give them some conflicting guidance.

In Matthew 6, Jesus says, "The world is full of so-called prayer warriors who are prayer-ignorant. They're full of formulas and programs and advice, peddling techniques for getting what you want from God. Don't fall for that nonsense. This is your Father you are dealing with, and he knows better than you what you need" (Matthew 6:7–8, MSG). Just one chapter later, Jesus says, "Don't bargain with God. Be direct. Ask for what you need. This isn't a cat-and mouse, hide-and-seek game we're in" (Matthew 7:7–8, MSG). So if God knows what we need better than we do, why do we need to ask for it?

Richard Rohr lists some of the misconceptions many of us have about what prayer is and is not:

> Are we trying to talk God into things? Does the group with the best prayers win? Is [a] prayer of petition just another way to get what we want? Or is it to get God on our side. In every case, notice that we are trying to take control.[1]

God is not a cosmic vending machine. We can't put in just the right prayer so that God will dispense what we want (stuff, healing, answers). So why does Jesus tell us to ask for what we want?

Rohr continues:

> We ask not to change God but to change ourselves. We pray to form a living relationship, not to get things done ... Prayer is not a way to try to control God, or even to get what we want. As Jesus says in Luke's Gospel the answer to every prayer is one, the same, and the best: the Holy Spirit! (See Luke 11:13.) God gives power more than answers.[2]

God is always more interested in having an honest conversation with us than in simply providing what we need. Many times we already have what we need and know the answers to our questions. Shortcomings like pride and impatience hide the truth from us. When we hand it all over to God with no strings attached, God takes it from us and backfills with the Holy Spirit to guide us, strengthen us, and empower us.

Unfortunately, it's human nature to think that we need to tell God not only what we want and need, but also to tell God how to provide it. That's why we spent so much time on steps 4 through 6. That's where humility comes in.

I'm Proud of My Humility!

The main objective of step 7 is to get out of ourselves and try to live as God wills for us. This is spiritual growth. This growth is not a result of wishing things were different. This is a result of action and prayer.

Becoming humble and asking God's help. That's step 7.

Humility is hard. It is counter-cultural and demands that we turn our back on everything that our present culture values. Our culture places short term gratification above concern for long-term well-being. It struggles to feed appetites that only grow greater as they are satisfied—appetites for money, possessions, and prestige. In the institutional church that looks like bigger budgets, larger congregations, and mega-buildings.

Humility renounces those values. However, those institutional values will remain a source of temptation and self-deception. We will not abandon our commitment to "make disciples for the transformation of the world," but we need to recognize that we will struggle to rise above the temptation to go back to the old ways.

So what does this "humility" look like? We may not be familiar with it.

This humility wreaks havoc with individualistic values. It means accepting and taking responsibility for the things that happen in life. (More on that in the next step.)

Humility is the laying aside of selfishness, self-ambition, personal prestige, and self-display. It is pushing back the temptation to be admired and respected, letting go of the temptation to have our opinion sought after, to be known by name, to be flattered.

We need to travel from being victims of pride and selfishness to thinking of others first. We need to give up self-reliance and move from self-centeredness to selflessness. If we concentrate on ourselves, we eliminate others.

Humility doesn't follow a set of rules or develop a set of personal qualities but is able to develop a heart of love and forgiveness. Humility is flexible; it is not always right.

True humility doesn't keep track of good works but focuses on change. Good works glorify God, not individuals. Simple acts of service, thinking of others first = humility.

Humility has no self-image to maintain. It has no need to look good to others. It does not hide its sin from others, but lays it out for all to see. We tend to be too hard on ourselves. Sharing our stories with others helps us to realize our shortcomings, as well as those of others and to live together toward recovery. To live without fault is not the purpose of Christian life. To live above reproach is not the goal. The goal is to humbly share the journey to recovery in community.

Humility only happens through prayer. Through prayer, God gives us the power to overcome our shortcomings.

Step 7

Hi, I'm Gerri! Hi, I'm Stan! We're churchaholics. We humbly asked God to remove our shortcomings and renew our spirits.

The name of this step is HUMILITY.

A daily and chosen "attitude of gratitude" will keep your hands open to expect life, allow life, and receive life at ever-deeper levels of satisfaction—but never to think you deserve it.

—Richard Rohr, *Breathing Under Water*

Something to Think About ...

To pray is to be willing to change.

- *How can you change your attitude and prayer life to reflect the change you want to become?*
- *What can you do today to deny yourself something in order that another might have what they need? Perhaps this means denying a thought or emotion in order to offer grace to another. Needs are not only physical.*

Endnotes

[1] Richard Rohr. *Breathing Under Water: Spirituality and the Twelve Steps*, St. Anthony Messenger Press, 2011 (Kindle).
[2] Ibid.

Become Willing

*We made a list of all persons and groups we had harmed,
and became willing to make amends to them all.*

Step 8 could be described as a condensed version of steps 4 through 6. In step 8, we make a list of those we have harmed through our addiction. Our fearless spiritual inventory from step 4 is a good place to start. Then we share our lists to make sure we haven't missed anyone or any group, consciously or unconsciously. Sharing our lists is very much like what we did in step 5. It keeps us honest. Finally, we ready ourselves to take action. We become willing (like step 6) to make amends, to make an honest attempt to acknowledge, and try to make up for, the harm we had done to others through our addiction to the institutional church and institutionalized religion.

Following the twelve steps is more like walking a loop trail than hiking from point "A" to point "B." We find ourselves covering the same ground over and over, as we struggle to avoid "falling off the wagon" and returning to our addiction.

Makin' a List ...

"We made a list of all persons and groups we had harmed."

Let's start with our fearless spiritual inventory of shortcomings:

- As professional clergy, we stepped in to do the ministry of the people in order to have ministry to report. We bought into the "score sheet."
- We backed off on presenting and living out the gospel as the gospel to avoid conflict, please others, and keep the church from going broke. Please note that we're not talking about harming others by hurting their feelings. Presenting the gospel honestly will always hurt feelings. Human arrogance and ignorance make hurt feelings inevitable. Ask Jesus! We presented the gospel honestly, but we failed to live out the gospel, no matter what.
- We delayed our departure from the institutional church out of fear of the unknown and fear of change.

Our initial reaction to this list of shortcomings was that we were the only ones harmed. We then jumped quickly into victim mode, i.e., we were pushed out of the church, "they" should be making amends to us! It's really easy to go there, even though we know better. Richard Rohr cautions,

> Step 8 is quite programmed, concrete, and specific. "Make a list," it says, and that list is of those *we* have harmed." Note that it does not say those who have harmed us, which will just get us back into the self-serving victim role.[1]

We needed to seriously consider the downstream victims of our shortcomings and name them.

1. When we did the ministry of the people, we shielded the congregation from the truth about their discipleship. By not allowing the ministries to fail, we may have denied others the oppor-

tunity to revive a ministry or start a new ministry. Certainly, we didn't develop any leaders by doing the ministries for them.

2. It's very expensive to keep a church on life support. Resources are wasted on keeping the institution alive. The church's mission of making disciples and transforming the culture fades into the background. We all become victims when this happens.

3. Delaying our departure from the institutional church victimized us and, by extension, our families and friends. The last three years were particularly difficult as we persisted in tweaking the rules, rituals, and traditions of the institutional church. Albert Einstein is frequently credited with saying, "The definition of insanity is doing the same thing over and over again and expecting a different result." We were not doing exactly the same things, but we were only tweaking. We were not able to overcome institutional resistance to change and make the very significant and foundational changes necessary to achieve different results.

Checkin' It Twice...

As hard as it sometimes is, we all need the strength, support, and accountability that a community offers. It's easy to lie to, and fool, ourselves; that's what addicts do. We need the help of people we can trust to tell us the truth, even when it hurts...especially when it hurts. Remember step 5?

The Narcotics Anonymous (NA) movement has been built on the same steps and the same process as the Alcoholics Anonymous (AA) movement. In its *Big Book*, NA offers this advice on how community works in support of this step:

> Listening carefully to other members share
> their experience regarding this step can relieve

any confusion that we may have about writing our list. Also, our sponsors may share with us how Step 8 worked for them. Asking a question during a meeting can give us the benefit of group conscience.[2]

What Are You Prepared to Do?

"We became willing to make amends to all persons and groups we had harmed."

What do Jesus and Sean Connery have in common? They both have the insight and the courage to challenge us with the question we need to hear, at exactly the moment we need to hear it. How are they different? Sean Connery is an actor, Jesus is not. In the movie *The Untouchables*, Connery, as he lies on the floor, bleeding to death, asks Elliott Ness (Kevin Costner), "What are you prepared to do?" Jesus asks the man who's been waiting at the healing pool in Jerusalem for thirty-eight years, "Do you want to be well?"

Both are really asking the same question, "What's it worth to you? You can be who God created you to be. You can be healed and whole. But you have to give up control and let God take over."

So how bad do you want the freedom and peace that God has promised? What are you prepared to do? Do you want to be well?

Richard Rohr said:

> We all need to do some clean-up work inside. For humans, there is only a slow softening of the heart, a gradual lessening of our attachment to our hurts, our victimhood as a past identity, or any need to punish or humiliate others. "Vengeance is mine,' says the Lord" (Romans 12:19). Vengeance against self or vengeance against anything is not our job. It might take a

long time to "become willing" to make amends, and that is why some people go to Step 8 meetings for years.[3]

We must really be willing to make amends. Really! Tempting as it might be to rush through these steps … *don't*! Only when you're prepared to do whatever it takes … only when you truly want to be well, should you move on to step 9.

Step 8

Hi, I'm Gerri! Hi, I'm Stan! We're churchaholics. We made a list of all persons and groups we had harmed, and became willing to make amends to them all.

The name of this step is RESPONSIBILITY.

This is how I want you to conduct yourself in these matters. If you enter your place of worship and about to make an offering, you suddenly remember a grudge a friend has against you, abandon your offering, leave immediately, go to this friend and make things right. Then and only then, come back and work things out with God (Matthew 5:23–24, MSG).

Something to Think About …

Sometimes the things that we neglect to do hurt others as much as the things that we do.

- *What are the situations in your life that point to both neglect and action that have harmed others?*

- *Who can you share this with that will hold you accountable to do what's necessary to move on?*

Endnotes

1. Richard Rohr. *Breathing Under Water: Spirituality and the Twelve Steps*, St. Anthony Messenger Press, 2011 (Kindle).
2. Narcotics Anonymous World services, Inc., *Twelve Steps and Twelve Traditions*, 6th Edition, Chatsworth CA, 2008, page 39.
3. Richard Rohr, *Breathing Under Water: Spirituality and the Twelve Steps*, St. Anthony Messenger Press, 2011 (Kindle).

Step 9

Make Amends

We made direct amends to all persons and groups we had harmed wherever possible, except when to do so would injure them or others.

"Ready, willing, and *able*" we humbly begin the hard work of step 9: making amends. If we have intentionally and honestly made our way through steps 4 through 8, we will be *able* to do this.

Richard Rohr says, "Step 9 is telling us how to use skillful means to both protect our own humanity and to liberate the humanity of others. It also says that our amends to others should be 'direct,' that is, specific, personal, and concrete, in other words, probably not an e-mail or a tweet."[1]

By "skillful means," Rohr means common sense wisdom. Discernment is the key to successfully making amends. We need to be able to discern when it is possible to make amends and when our attempts to make amends would only serve to injure those we have harmed or others. In order to do that, we need to understand the spiritual condition of those we are making amends to. We need to "walk a mile in their shoes."

Rohr continues, "One often needs time, discernment, and good advice from others before one knows *the when, how, who, and where* to apologize or make amends. If not done skillfully, an apology can actually make the problem and the hurt worse ... Not everything needs to be told to everybody, all the time, and in full detail. Sometimes it only increases the hurt, the problem, and the person's inability to forgive. This all takes wise discernment and often sought-out advice from others."[2]

When, How, Who, and Where

Determining when to make amends requires a fine sense of timing. We have to balance between taking advantage of opportunities when they present themselves, rushing to make amends and thereby causing more harm, and our natural tendency to procrastinate. Timing is everything; don't rush it, but don't put it off indefinitely either. Pray for guidance and listen to the Holy Spirit, you'll know when it's the right time to make amends.

Clearly, amends need to be made face-to-face whenever possible. With modern technology, even when we can't meet with someone face-to-face for practical reasons like being far apart, we can have a virtual face-to-face meeting on our computers or smart phones. Having a telephone conversation is acceptable when a face-to-face meeting is simply not possible. You may want to write out what you intend to say.

We made a list of persons and groups that we had harmed in step 8, but others may be identified as we make amends to those on our list. We should be open and willing to add names to our list as they come up. However, it is quite possible that some persons will claim we hurt their feelings. As we noted in step 8, hurt feelings do not necessarily constitute harm. The Gospel of Jesus Christ will inevitably hurt the feelings of those it convicts. The Apostle Peter's feelings were hurt when Jesus called him "Satan" and again when Jesus challenged Peter's faith in a storm on the sea, and again when he denied Jesus three times and Jesus just stared at him. Jesus hurt Peter's feelings to save Peter's life.

Amends can be made publicly or privately. Normally, amends should be made privately and face-to-face unless a group has been harmed. Richard Rohr cautions us about making amends publicly:

> We have a myth of "total disclosure" in our culture that is not always fair or even helpful. Just because it is factually true, does not mean everyone can handle it or even needs to handle it, or has a right to the information.
>
> What people want to hear in salacious and gossipy detail has now been fed by our media-saturated society, and our wanting to know has become our right to know. Gossip is not a right but a major obstacle to human love and spiritual wisdom. Paul lists it equally with the much more grievous "hot sins" (Romans 1:29–31), and yet most of us do it rather easily.[3]

That said, our addiction to the institutional church and institutionalized religion will require us to make some of our amends publicly. As the Narcotics Anonymous *Big Book* says, "Sometimes the only way we can make amends is to contribute to society. Now we are helping ourselves and other addicts to recover. This is a tremendous amend to the whole community."[4]

It's Your Choice ... Entirely up to You

We made amends to those we may have prevented from developing as leaders and Jesus-followers by being transparent and non-competitive. We offered to meet face-to-face with anyone in the congregation we served who wanted to talk about our departure from the church. When we met with people, we apologized where appropriate for doing the ministry that was rightly their ministry to do. We told them of our plans to start a new faith community outside the institutional church and emphasized that they could choose to stay, choose to go, or both. We told them that our new community would not gather on Sunday morning or compete in any way with the institutional church.

Some of those we talked to have stayed with the institutional church, some have joined our new community, some are doing both. A few have stepped away from "church" altogether.

We had several meetings with the pastor who replaced us. We worked very hard to be completely transparent about the state of the church and told him of our plans. Since retiring, we have stayed away from the church, from the denominational authorities who forced our retirement, and from those in the congregation who could not accept the changes needed to transform the church.

We recognized that our addiction had harmed our own spirituality. Through our work with the recovery community and our training in pastoral counseling, we knew that "part of learning how to live successfully is learning when we need help."[5] A trusted mental health professional advised us to avoid all contact, to the extent possible, with the denominational and local church people who had opposed our ministry. We have followed that advice and made amends to ourselves by giving ourselves time to heal.

follow ~ a community

We made amends to the "whole community" by establishing a movement of Jesus-followers. *follow ~ a community* is an alternative to the institutional church and institutionalized religion. For tax purposes, *follow* is a 501c(3) tax exempt church … but only for tax purposes! We are a community, not a traditional church. We do not own a building. We do not worship on Sunday, we gather on Saturday. We are community co-leaders, not pastors in the traditional sense. We prefer to be called Jesus-followers, not Christians.

*follow is a nurturing community that gathers to follow Jesus
by praying, learning, and caring for others*

follow is a movement, not an institution. We believe that the
first community of Jesus-followers described in the Bible is still the
model for faith communities:

> They committed themselves to the teach-
> ing of the apostles, the life together, the common
> meal, and the prayers. All the believers lived in
> wonderful harmony, holding everything in com-
> mon. They sold whatever they owned and pooled
> their resources so that each person's need was
> met. They followed a daily discipline of worship
> in the Temple followed by meals at home, every
> meal a celebration, exuberant and joyful, as they
> praised God. (Acts 2:42, 44–46, MSG)

We realize that the first-century community described in Acts
cannot be replicated in the twenty-first century, but it is an excellent model to emulate. There are a number of excellent resources
available to help build a community of Jesus-followers. We have
chosen to use *Called to Community: The Life Jesus Wants for His
People*, compiled and edited by Charles E. Moore, as our primary
guide.

A few months after *follow* began gathering weekly as a community, we began to sense that we were sliding off the wagon, so
to speak. We were beginning to default to the traditional worship
services that we had left on Sunday morning. For some reason, be
it comfort level, energy level, or just a lapse in attentiveness, our
Saturday gathering was starting to feel like Sunday morning worship. We were again feeling less connected to God and others and
more compelled to meet the expectations of ourselves and others to
provide a certain kind of worship experience. Just a change of venue,

from sanctuary to living room was not the experience we intended. That was tweaking.

We took some time during the next gathering to talk it out as a family of believers. Following a somewhat emotional and affirming discussion, we regained our footing as a movement and everyone vowed to stay alert for signs that we were getting off track and falling into the "we've always done it this way before" trap. We renewed our commitment to continually explore "how we can be Jesus in this community, for one another, and for the world."

Obedience Is Thicker than Blood

We made amends to our families and friends for our delayed departure from the institutional church. They suffered with us, as our pride and fear kept us chained to a system that refused to change and drained our spirituality.

We realized that our families were not necessarily called to be part of a new movement of Jesus-followers, so we offered them the same options we offered other members of the congregation: leave, stay, or both. We stressed that they were under no obligation to leave the denomination or local church, and we assured them that they were under no obligation to be part of *follow - a community*.

Family can be, and often is, one of the biggest impediments to living a life centered on Jesus. Jesus himself was confronted with the difficult choice of living out his call against the wishes of his family:

> While he was still talking to the crowd, his mother and brothers showed up. They were outside trying to get a message to him. Someone told Jesus, "Your mother and brothers are out here, wanting to speak with you."
>
> Jesus didn't respond directly, but said, "Who do you think my mother and brothers are?" He

then stretched out his hand toward his disciples. "Look closely. These are my mother and brothers. Obedience is thicker than blood. The person who obeys my heavenly Father's will is my brother and sister and mother" (Matthew 12:46–50, MSG).

Many Bible scholars believe that Jesus's mother and brothers were there to talk him out of this "God has anointed me to bring good news to the poor and set the captives free" nonsense. His life and their family's reputation were at stake.

As soon as you know that you must follow Jesus and go "all in" for God, it's best to let those closest to you know. Procrastinating only prolongs their pain as they make decisions about their own spiritual journey.

James A. Garfield says, "The truth will set you free, but first it will make you miserable." Step 9 is about stepping up and stepping out. It's about becoming accountable for what we have said and done.

Step 9

Hi, I'm Gerri! Hi, I'm Stan! We're churchaholics. We made direct amends to all persons and groups we had harmed wherever possible, except when to do so would injure them or others.

The name of this step is ACCOUNTABILITY.

Patience is an important part of our recovery. The unconditional love we experience will rejuvenate our will to live, and each positive move on our part will be matched by an unexpected opportunity. A lot of courage and faith goes into making an amend, and a lot of spiritual growth results.

—Narcotics Anonymous World Services,
Twelve Steps and Twelve Traditions

Something to Think About ...

Harming another person means that you have somehow kept that person from being all that he/she can be. This could have been due to physical harm, emotional stress, or financial abuse.

- *Realizing that harming others and hurting their feelings is not the same, make a list of those you have harmed.*
- *Can you think of how you could make amends to each of them? Are you willing to do that?*

Endnotes

1. Richard Rohr, *Breathing Under Water: Spirituality and the Twelve Steps*, St. Anthony Messenger Press, 2011 (Kindle).
2. Ibid.
3. Ibid.
4. Narcotics Anonymous World Services, Inc., *Twelve Steps and Twelve Traditions*, 6th Edition, Chatsworth CA, 2008, page 41.
5. Ibid, page 40.

Step 10

Daily Inventory

We continued to make a searching and fearless daily spiritual inventory and promptly admitted our failures and shortcomings.

As we have mentioned before, this recovery stuff is not a "once and done" program. It's a way of life. There is no straight line between addiction and recovery; it's a continuous loop. All of the twelve steps are worked, all the time, not in any real order. Just as we cannot separate our physical being from our spiritual being, we cannot isolate the steps, one from another.

Step 10 is preventative action. When we work this step continuously, it helps us to monitor our feelings, our fantasies, and our actions, one day at a time. It's easy to think that "we have arrived." But old habits die hard and unless we continually evaluate and take inventory of our lives we will become ensnared in old traps, and return to old habits. The daily review helps us keep from backsliding.

When things are going well, we tend to forget how vital it is to come to God through a daily review. All it takes is a minor struggle or a bad day to draw us back into our old familiar patterns of addictive behavior.

Ministry is hard, often thankless, work. It is difficult to remain emotionally neutral when others are questioning or criticizing your every move. We needed to be able to step back and observe what we were experiencing and how we reacted to provocations. We could not control how others acted, but we could control how we reacted. Taking an inventory of the day, and our reaction to all the day held for us, helped keep us on track.

This step is similar to step 4. The purpose of step 4 is to determine the causes and conditions of our addiction and to assess where we are spiritually. If we are to continue to recover from our addiction to rules, rituals, and traditions we must review over and over again what led us to the addiction, how it manifests itself, and how we can stay on the road to recovery.

Step 5 is about sharing our inventory with another person whom we trust. We need to do that as often as possible in step 10 as well. Community is essential to this process. We're all in this together.

It's easy to be hard on ourselves. We need to realize that all rules, rituals, and traditions are not "bad" for us. However, our focus on them, and worship of them, had led us away from God. We must be careful to avoid getting back on that path. The daily review keeps us aware that our recovery has led us toward God. It helps us learn to follow Jesus day-to-day.

Daily repetition allows us to be more open to God. It allows us to move closer to God in thought and deed, and to open our hearts more fully to God's will.

The Daily

We accomplish this daily review by means of a small prayer known as The Examen of Consciousness.[1] It is a prayer developed by St. Ignatius of Loyola and his followers. The prayer helps us step back and look at ourselves, our actions, attitudes, and relationships. It acts as a spiritual guide as we come before God each day and examine our life, one day at a time.

First, we become aware of God's presence:

We recognize and recall that we are always in the presence of God, but we intentionally place ourselves in God's presence as we ask the Holy Spirit to help us look at our life this day.

Second, we review the day with gratitude:

We give thanks for the day and the gifts it has brought to us. We take care to notice what we gave and what we received.

Third, we pay attention to our emotions:

We look at the way we have responded to God's gracious gifts and to God's love. We do not judge our response but ask for help in understanding our responses.

Fourth, we review the entire day:

We pay attention to the context of what happened, how we acted, our motives and feelings. We take inventory. When were we at our best? When was there a barrier to God's presence? How conscious were we to God's presence in the situation?

Then we notice our daily habits and ask ourselves, "When did I give genuine charity and love?"

If I did not ... why not?

We determine if our daily habits, our ways of thinking and reacting, and the people we surround ourselves with are causing us to be negative. If that is the case, we ask God to help us turn the negative to positive.

Reviewing the day helps us examine our action and reactions. It helps us avoid excuses and rationalization. We can admit our mistakes to God. We don't have to explain them.

We ask God for forgiveness, to be with us in all situations. We ask for guidance. We thank God for the grace shown to us through others.

Finally, we just let our hearts talk to God:

We acknowledge that we will never be perfect. We accept God's grace and allow ourselves the freedom to be ourselves. We ask for what we need for tomorrow and again give thanks for what today brought our way.

Searching and Fearless

October 23, 2015, was a day we won't soon forget. We were attending the Future of the Church Summit at Group Publishing in Loveland, Colorado. We were listening to a panel of speakers explain new ways of being the old church when the Holy Spirit took over and forced us to take a hard look at our lives and our ministry.

Our searching and fearless inventory for that day went something like this:

When John White tearfully challenged us to stop "tweaking" the church model that we had grown up with and risk leaving the institution to start a movement of Jesus-followers, we knew that we had heard from the Spirit. We knew that we were in *God's presence.*

During the Summit closing worship, we *gave thanks* for the revelation we had received and made a commitment to share our experience with our families, our friends, and our brothers and sisters in the church we served.

We carefully *examined our emotions* to make sure we were not overreacting to John's tears or our own sense of frustration with the rules, rituals, and traditions that were holding us captive. There was a kind of "watershed" moment when we knew beyond a shadow of a doubt that the church and our own spirituality could not be resurrected unless they died first.

As we *reviewed the events of the day,* we realized that we had experienced freedom from our addiction. We had relaxed our need to be in control, to fill out the checklist, to be perfect. The Spirit gave us permission to relax and just be with God. We realized that by letting God be God we became the persons God created us to be.

We admitted our pride and impatience to God. We admitted that we could not make people care. We admitted that we could not come up with the perfect program that would bring people to God. We admitted that we were more about worshipping Jesus than following Jesus.

Then we sat in silence for a long time and *listened to God*. We asked God to give us what we needed for the next day, and honestly prayed for God's will to be done in us.

Step 10

Hi, I'm Gerri! Hi, I'm Stan! We're churchaholics. We continued to make a searching and fearless daily spiritual inventory and promptly admitted our failures and shortcomings.

The name of this step is AWARENESS.

Jesus said, "So don't worry about tomorrow, for tomorrow will bring its own worries. Today's trouble is enough for today" (Matthew 6:34, NLT, Jesus-Centered Bible).

Something to Think About …

Daily prayer and meditation keep us accountable to God and provide a "daily review" of our lives.

- *What spiritual practice or "check in" with God helps keep your prayer life on track?*
- *If you don't currently have a daily habit of spiritual review, what might motivate you to begin one?*

Endnote

[1.] IgnatianSpirituality.com, a service of Loyola Press.

Part 3

Coming Home

Be still, and know that I am God!

—Yahweh
Psalm 46:10 (NLT, Jesus-Centered Bible)

Be still, *be calm, see,* and understand I am the True God.
I AM
—*Psalm 46:10 (The Voice)*

Step out of the traffic! Take a long,
loving look at me, your high God,
above politics, above everything.
—God, *Psalm 46:10 (The Message)*

Pray and Meditate

*We sought through prayer and meditation to improve our
conscious contact with God, praying only for knowledge
of God's will for us and the power to carry that out.*

We performed a daily inventory to sustain and continue our recovery in step 10. Step 10 reminds us daily of our shortcomings and failures so that we can acknowledge them and begin to correct them right away, before they drag us back into our addiction. In the same way, step 11 sustains our recovery by continually connecting us with the source of our strength, energy, and direction for recovery: God. Prayer and meditation are how we connect with God.

We Need to Talk!

To pray is to change. When we genuinely pray, the real condition of our heart is revealed. That is when God begins to work within us. The purpose of step 11 is to increase our awareness of God's presence in our lives and thereby develop a relationship with God. It is from this relationship that we gain a source of strength for our continuing recovery, our new life.

We think of prayer as "talking to God." It is more than that, but we'll go with that definition for now. Meditation is listening to God. The daily practice of both can help promote emotional balance and stability.

We, like many Americans, pray for what *we* desire. We pray for things to go our way, for our plans to come to fruition, for our financial success, for our children to get an education and a good job, for a positive outcome on a health issue. We pray to the Santa Claus god. This is the god that grants our wishes. This is not the God of the Bible. When our prayers are not answered in our time, to our satisfaction, we decide that God wasn't listening or didn't hear our prayer. We might come to believe that God is not real.

That is *not* how prayer works. We experience God's answers and direction when we seek God's will for our life and not our own will. Through prayer and meditation we find it easier to discern God's will from our own, and act and think accordingly.

We had tried to run our lives on the basis of our will power alone. Oh sure, we had a discipline of daily prayer and would perfunctorily pray and ask God's guidance, but for the most part, we just wanted confirmation of our own decisions and direction. Then of course there were the prayers of desperation that went up as a last resort, when we felt helpless. That did not go so well. It is when we deliberately give up control that prayer becomes effective.

Jesus said this about praying:

> And when you come before God, don't turn that into a theatrical production either. All these people making a regular show out of their prayers, hoping for stardom! Do you think God sits in a box seat?
>
> Here's what I want you to do: Find a quiet, secluded place so you won't be tempted to role-play before God. Just be there as simply and hon-

estly as you can manage. The focus will shift from you to God, and you will begin to sense his grace.

The world is full of so-called prayer warriors who are prayer ignorant. They're full of formulas and programs and advice, peddling techniques for getting what you want from God. Don't fall for that nonsense. This is your Father you are dealing with, and he knows better than you what you need. (Matthew 6:5–13, MSG)

We don't pray to look good, to fulfill the daily checklist or to impress others. Luke 17:21 tells us that the kingdom of God is within us. What comes from our heart reaches the heart of God. The first step of prayer is to simply be ourselves and come humbly before God. Prayer changes us from the inside. The kingdom of God works in human hearts. It produces new people. We need to simply speak from our hearts.

It is hard work to learn to pray and it takes practice. Many of us are intimidated by prayer. We believe that we have to wait … until our motives are pure, until we can use the correct words, until we know enough, until we are spiritually prepared, and so on. But it is when we simply start praying, that we tune into God's presence and begin the relationship. Just like any other relationship, we can't build on something we don't pay attention to. Praying and meditating is paying attention to God … all the time.

Our prayers are just what they are. We make no pretense. We begin where we are because where we are is holy ground. We open our hearts: make requests, share concerns, and petition God to help others. We carry on an ongoing conversation about the stuff of our lives sharing our hurts, sorrows, and joys. We don't need to sort it all out. God does that.

We can give God the good, the bad and the ugly of each day. In talking to God about what's really going on inside us, we sense relief, even if it is something that we think might displease God. God knows us better than we know ourselves. We can't hide from God.

We can complain, argue, and yell. We give to God what is in us, not what "should" be in us. God can take it. The prophet Jeremiah gives God a good dressing down in chapter 20 of his book. He exclaims that God has made him a laughing stock, a household joke, and he is not happy. God continued to use Jeremiah and God will continue to use us; mostly when we don't like it!

To hunger for God is to pray. At first, we are the focus of our prayers. As we continue to practice the discipline of prayer our focus will shift. We slowly move from being the center of our prayer to having God at the center. We realize that we are part of God's plan, not that God is part of our life plan. We continually pray that we live according to God's will for our life.

Shut Up and Listen

We move from a time of talking to God to a time of listening to God speak to us. This rarely happens in an audible fashion. It's in the stillness of our hearts that the Holy Spirit speaks the loudest. It is in the quiet waiting that God gives us answers and nudges us to action. In order to hear God, we need to be quiet. Stan's dad often shared this homespun wisdom, "You can't hear with your mouth open."

This time of listening is called meditation. It's a time to be still and become self-aware. Like prayer, it can be difficult and must be practiced regularly.

In times of quiet, it becomes evident that we are also addicted to "doing." Our minds can generate all kinds of excuses to do something instead of just being quiet, open, and present. Our "being" and our "doing" are at war.

It can be difficult to sit and wait for God. We will have distractions. There are times when we cannot settle down and still our minds. We may try to use images or music that actually keep us from being present to God. We would rather not notice the things going on within us. Concerns, worry over insignificant things, our competitive nature, and our self-importance can get in the way of truly listening to God.

There are things that meditation will bring to mind that we may be happy to ignore. We like being in charge of our lives. We may not want to hear what God has to say to us or ask of us. We may want to avoid the discomfort of being still because it has not become comfortable for us. But it will, if we keep at it. We need to continue to practice prayer and meditation. The fact that we may fail, again and again, is no excuse to quit trying.

Helpful Hints

Prayer and meditation tips, guides, and techniques can help, but they are not prayer or meditation unless one's heart is connected to God. We have listed some things that help us connect:

- Paul tells the Thessalonians to "never stop praying" (1 Thessalonians 5:16, NLT, Jesus-Centered Bible). That seems like a tall order, until you begin to make God the center of your life. The more we converse with God, the more natural it becomes to consult with God throughout the day, even when conversing with others. If you approach prayer as a continuing conversation with your BFF (best friend forever), it becomes much easier to never stop praying. Don't think of prayer as something you do at a certain time, in a certain place, or in a particular way; think of prayer as a lifestyle.
- We cannot overestimate the importance of beginning and ending each day with prayer and meditation. That's how Jesus prayed. We also pray before each meal, at home or in a restaurant. There's a mysterious spiritual connection that happens when we gather around a meal. In addition, we use this brief prayer when we shower in the morning:

Lord, wash me with your grace, fill me
with your Spirit, renew my soul.
May I live today as your child.
May I bring you honor and glory by serving your other children
as the hands, feet, and voice of Jesus.
Your will be done.

When we bathe we remember our "baptism" and we re-baptize ourselves with water and God's love. Richard Rohr says, "Love is endlessly alive, always flowing toward the lower place, and thus life-giving for all, exactly like water. In fact, there is no form of life that does not need water. No wonder water is such a universal spiritual symbol."[1]

- Most of us are afraid of silence. We have noticed that people start getting nervous after only one minute of silence, even in worship. When the prophet Elijah was running for his life and hiding in a cave, God taught him a lesson we all need to learn. First, there was a mighty windstorm, but God wasn't in the windstorm. Then, there was a huge earthquake, but God wasn't in the earthquake. Then, there was a roaring fire, but God wasn't in the fire. Finally, there was a gentle whisper. God was in the whisper. The God of the whisper gave Elijah strength, courage, and direction.[31] Don't hide in the noise; find God in the silence. Start with a few minutes and work your way up. After five years of practice, we usually begin a spiritual retreat or time of meditation with at least thirty minutes of silence.

- Find a way to let the distractions and uninvited thoughts go away when praying and meditating. Our brains want to work 24-7. We can't shut our brains off, but we can learn to let stuff go so that we can focus in on God. Some say to let those anxious thoughts (How will Peter react to my e-mail?), worries (How will those medical tests turn out?), concerns (I hope Paul gets his life turned around.), scheduling issues

(When will I find time to finish that paper?), etc. go, by imagining them on a TV screen just passing through. That hasn't worked for us. Instead, we imagine ourselves placing all those thoughts, worries, concerns, and issues in a boat and letting them go downstream in the river's current, floating away. Find your own metaphor, but find one. Distractions and uninvited thoughts will prevent you from connecting to God.

Step 10 takes us back to step 4 as we sustain the progress we've made and continue our recovery journey in community. Step 11 takes us back to "square one." Step 11 takes us home, home to God. Through prayer and meditation, we continue to build our relationship with God. Through prayer and meditation, we rediscover, daily and even hourly, that we can't overcome our addiction, that God can, and that God will, if we surrender our will. Step 11 takes us back to steps 1 through 3: I can't, God can, let God. Wait on the Lord.

This earth is not our home. We're only here on a work visa. Our home is not just with God. God is our home. When was the last time you were home?

Step 11

Hi, I'm Gerri! Hi, I'm Stan! We're churchaholics. We sought through prayer and meditation to improve our conscious contact with God, praying only for knowledge of God's will for us and the power to carry that out.

The name of this step is PATIENCE.

Jesus went on a little farther and bowed with his face to the ground, praying, "My Father! If it is possible, let this cup of suffering be taken away from me. Yet I want your will to be done, not mine" (Matthew 26:39, NLT, Jesus-Centered Bible).

Something to Think About ...

It is said that praying is talking with God and meditation is listening as God talks to us.

It is in silence that we often hear God nudge us toward action. That can be uncomfortable, because the action is usually something we would rather not do.

- *When was the last time God asked you to do something that was uncomfortable or inconvenient? What was it? Did you do it?*

Endnotes

[1] Richard Rohr, *Eager to Love: The Alternative Way of Francis of Assisi*, Franciscan Media, 2014, pages 267–268.

[2] 1 Kings 19:1–18.

Part 4

Sharing Recovery

The opposite of addiction is not sobriety.
The opposite of addiction is connection.

—Johann Hari,
TED Talks

Give It Away

*Having had a spiritual awakening as a result of these
steps, we tried to carry this message to all those addicted to
religious institutions and institutionalized religion, and
to practice these principles in all aspects of our lives.*

Step 12 is not the final step … it's just step 12. We continually and simultaneously work all of the steps. Step 12 brings us into community so that all might be encouraged and strengthened by the practices. Discovering who Jesus is, and how to live as he lived, can only be done in community. The twelve steps are intended to form a pattern for our day-to-day life together.

Our commitment is solidified when we share our experiences with others. In fact, our own recovery will not be complete until it is shared. Practical experience shows that nothing will ensure immunity from institutionalized religion so much as intensive work with others who are done with the institutional church.[1]

Jesus himself promises to live this journey with us: "Go out and train everyone you meet, far and near, in this way of life, marking them by baptism in the three-fold name: Father, Son, and Holy Spirit. Then instruct them in the practice of all I have commanded you. I'll be with you as you do this, day after day after day, right up to the end of the age" (Matthew 28:19–20, MSG).

We cannot live in isolation. We must live in community. It is by sharing with and caring for others that we are able to stay true to our center, following Jesus. When we share this life with others, our own lives are strengthened and our efforts to live as Jesus lived are affirmed. Jesus gives us the authority to teach, to coach, and to encourage others in the faith. Remember, we cannot do this on our own. We have the promise that the Holy Spirit is with us.

Our primary task is to help others recover their spirituality and become free of their addiction to institutionalized religion. We are to love God and our neighbor as we love ourselves. There is plenty to do. As we love and serve others there will be ample opportunity to share our recovery stories and our faith journey. This is where we experience the joy of helping others on their journey toward simply following Jesus. If you look out just for yourself you will never be happy or satisfied.

> If you want more happy than your heart will hold
> If you want to stand taller if the truth were told
> Take whatever you have, and give it away
> If you want less lonely and a lot more fun
> And deep satisfaction when the day is done
> Then throw your heart wide open and give it away[2]

By serving others, we serve Jesus ("I tell you the truth, when you did it to one of the least of these my brothers and sisters, you were doing it to me!" [Matthew 25:40, NLT, Jesus-centered Bible]). By serving others and serving with others, relationships are built. Trust is built. Opportunities will develop.

For those of us in recovery, helping others will be inconvenient. There are those who will want our time, anytime, perhaps all our time. We need to discern who is willing and able to be well. These are those we need to invest our time in. It is a waste of time to choose those who will not work with you. People must want help. This recovery journey is tough and there are no easy answers.

Don't rush it! When you discover someone who is done, or nearly done, with the institutional church, find out all you can about them. Listen to their story when they are ready to share it. If you find that they are not really serious about overcoming their addiction, don't waste time trying to persuade them. You may spoil a later opportunity.[3]

When Jesus sent his closest followers out to share the Good News of recovery he gave them some sage advice that we need to heed as well:

> Don't begin by traveling to some far-off place to convert unbelievers. And don't try to be dramatic by tackling some public enemy. Go to the lost, confused people right here in the neighborhood. Tell them that the kingdom is here. Bring health to the sick. Raise the dead. Touch the untouchables. Kick out the demons. You have been treated generously, so live generously. (Matthew 10:5–8, MSG)

Start close to home. In fact, start at home with your own family. Don't be dramatic, just explain the steps and how they have helped you overcome your addiction to the institution of the church. Describe the recovery of your spirituality and your discovery of Jesus. Pay it forward.

> When you knock on a door, be courteous in your greeting. If they welcome you, be gentle in your conversation. If they don't welcome you, quietly withdraw. Don't make a scene. Shrug your shoulders and be on your way. (Matthew 10:12–14, MSG)

Don't rush it. Don't push it. This may not be the right time and you may not be the right messenger.

Sharing recovery takes some finesse. Jesus told his followers to be "as cunning as a snake, inoffensive as a dove." This is hard, but essential work, for each of us. Remember, if you're not making disciples, you're not a disciple. Don't skip this step!

Step 12

Hi, I'm Gerri! Hi, I'm Stan! We're churchaholics. Having had a spiritual awakening as a result of these steps, we tried to carry this message to all those addicted to religious institutions and institutionalized religion, and to practice these principles in all aspects of our lives.

The name of this step is SERVICE.

Jesus said, "Let me tell you why you are here. You're here to be salt-seasoning that brings out the God flavors of this earth. If you lose your saltiness, how will people taste godliness? You've lost your usefulness and will end up in the garbage. Here's another way to put it: You're here to be light, bringing out the God-colors in the world. God is not a secret to be kept. We're going public with this, as public as a city on a hill. If I make you light-bearers, you don't think I'm going to hide you under a bucket, do you? I'm putting you on a light stand. Now that I've put you there on a hilltop, on a light stand—stand! Keep open house; be generous with your lives. By opening up to others, you'll prompt people to open up with god, this generous Father in heaven" (Matthew 5:13–16, MSG).

Something to Think About ...

If you tend to be a hermit, keep to yourself, and involve yourself in little activity outside of your own home or circle of friends, you will not experience spiritual growth. If you look out only for yourself you, will never be happy or satisfied.

- *Where could you connect with and serve others in your community? What prevents you from doing this?*
- *If you are not serving, what steps could you take to begin a life of service to others?*

Endnotes

[1.] Adapted from Alcoholics Anonymous World Services, *Big Book of Alcoholics Anonymous*, 4th Edition, 2001, page 89.
[2.] Alfie Zappacosta, Marco Luciani. Copyright © Sony/ATV Music Publishing LLC, Universal Music Publishing Group.
[3.] Adapted from Alcoholics Anonymous World Services. *Big Book of Alcoholics Anonymous*, 4th Edition, 2001, page 90.

Keep on Keepin' on

"Belief in the power of God, plus enough
willingness, honesty, and humility
to establish and maintain the new order of things,
were the essential requirements."

—Bill W., co-founder of AA,
Working the Steps

Recovering from church and discovering Jesus is a lifelong journey, not a destination. Addictions can only be treated, they cannot be cured. Ask any recovering alcoholic, they'll tell you that they will always be an alcoholic. In the same way, we will never lose our desire to connect with the God who created us. The twelve steps help us recover from trying to make that connection on our own power—through the rules, rituals, and traditions of the institutional church.

One of the great mysteries of our journey to connect with God is that God has always been there, waiting to connect with us. The twelve steps are designed to help us get out of our own way. "Hosanna" is not the same as "hallelujah" or its modern equivalent, "Way to go!" Hosanna is a cry for help. Hosanna means "Save us!" As Jesus entered Jerusalem on the Sunday before his crucifixion, the crowds cried, "Hosanna ... save us!" For addicts, the cry is often,

"Hosanna ... save us from ourselves!"

Remember the first three steps are: "I Can't," "God Can," "Let God." In William Paul Young's classic novel *The Shack*, the paradox of how we are always chasing after God, only to find that God (in

Jesus and the Holy Spirit) has been pursuing us all along, is described this way:

> Jesus said, "I have followers who were murderers and many who were self-righteous. Some are bankers and bookies, Americans and Iraqis, Jews and Palestinians. I have no desire to make them Christians, but I do want to join them in their transformation into sons and daughters of my Papa [God], into my brothers and sisters, into my Beloved."
>
> "Does that mean," said Mack, "that all roads will lead to you?"
>
> "Not at all." Jesus smiled as he reached for the door handle to the shop. "Most roads don't lead anywhere. What it does mean is that I will travel any road to find you."[1]

Mack was raised in the institutional church. He had memorized John 14:6 in Sunday school: "I am the way, the truth, and the life. No one can come to the Father except through me." The church had taught Mack to read that verse as exclusive. Jesus meant it to be inclusive of all humanity. We are all in this together and Jesus journeys with us. Mack had a lot to unlearn and so do we. God will travel any road to find each and every one of us. *I Can't … God Can … Let God.*

Patience

"The journey of a thousand miles begins with one step."

—Lao Tzu

As the old saying goes, "Rome wasn't built in a day." The institutional church and institutionalized religion have been around since the Roman Emperor Constantine presided over the "shotgun wedding" of the Christian church and the Empire, producing the Holy Roman Empire. That was seventeen centuries ago. Followers of Jesus have a lot of rules, rituals, and traditions to overcome.

Today, we live in a culture of instant gratification. We have little patience with patience. Remember when a large file could take hours to download on to your computer? Now we get impatient if it takes more than a few minutes. We often catch ourselves rushing from one place to another and from one task to another. Why? Where are we going in such a hurry? The Amish have a saying, "The hurrier I go, the behinder I get." There's a lot of truth in that.

Patience is difficult. It's not just waiting for something to happen over which we have no control. That would be like waiting for the rain to stop, the plane to land, or the return of a loved one. Patience is a process. Henry Nouwen says that "patience asks us to live the moment to the fullest, to be completely present to the moment, to taste the here and now, to be where we are." We often want to escape the here and now and move on ... NOW. Often patience allows us see the treasures that are here ... NOW!

Most of us have heard the old proverb, "Patience is a virtue." The Apostle Paul lists patience as a fruit of the Holy Spirit (Galatians 5:22–23). Overcoming our addiction to the institutional church and institutionalized religion will take time. If we surrender our will to God's will, the Spirit of God will help us to be patient. God will give us the time we need when we stop insisting on the time and date we want.

Six months after we retired from the institutional church to form a new community of Jesus-followers, we caught ourselves becoming impatient with our progress. We wanted results. We wanted our community to grow and multiply. We wanted those who gathered with us to be as committed to following Jesus as we are. In the midst of our impatience, we realized that we were trying to schedule the

Spirit's work. We were sliding "off the wagon" and we needed to work the steps.

We took about a month off from trying to grow a new community. We had to go all the way back to step 1 and acknowledge once again that we couldn't make people care, that we could not force them to follow Jesus. As we prayed and reflected, we were inspired by the story of two "church-planters" who moved to Denver to start a new faith community and spent their first two years listening and building relationships before gathering for the first time as a community.[2]

The irony is, the more we work the steps, the more patient we become. We become more patient with ourselves, more patient with others, and finally, more patient with God. When you feel yourself getting anxious to move on, rushing ahead ... STOP! The God who created time will give you the time you need. Take a breath, take a time-out, count to ten. God will never leave you behind.

Persistence

"Never, never, never give up."
—Winston Churchill

We often use "persistence" and "perseverance" interchangeably, but there is a difference. For example, a boxer who keeps getting up no matter how many times he or she is knocked down is persistent. A boxer who fights until the final bell, no matter how many rounds there are, perseveres. *Webster's* says that to persist is "to refuse to give up when faced with opposition or difficulty" and perseverance is "continued, patient effort."

Recovering from an addiction is hard work and often brings us into conflict with the culture that promotes the addiction. People will question your integrity and your intelligence. You will question yourself. You will be tempted to give up and revert to the comfort and convenience afforded by the institutional church. You will be tempted to blend back into the mainstream. You will be knocked down, but with God's help you will always be able to get back up.

Here are some of the "knock-downs" that we've experienced:

"Movements cannot be sustained without institutions."

"Why don't you move somewhere where people will appreciate *your* kind of ministry?"

"This new thing you're doing is not a *real* church."

"Why can't you just get along?"

"Let me introduce you to some *real* Christians."

"Here's some money. Buy some decent clothes."

Sometimes, we slipped and fell down:

"Are we making a difference?"

"We'll be the only ones there."

"No one is committed to following Jesus."

"No one really cares."

"Are we going to run out of money?"

All of us get discouraged at one time or another. Even Jesus occasionally got frustrated with his followers. That's where God and community come in. It's always easier to get back up after a knock-down with help from God and good friends. We don't need sympathy. We need empathy. Jesus was fully human. He can and will empathize with us. Those in our recovery community have experienced knockdowns themselves. They can empathize with us.

We'd have been toast without each other, our community, and God's grace. Maintaining connections with God (steps 1–3 and 11) and our community (steps 4–10 and 12) by working the steps is critical to recovery. There will be setbacks and knockdowns, count on it! When it comes to never giving up: "The opposite of addiction is not sobriety. The opposite of addiction is connection."[3]

Perseverance

"You simply have to put one foot in front
of the other and keep going."

—George Lucas

It's one thing to get knocked down and get back up. It's another to endure difficulty day after day after day … no drama, just dogged determination. Perseverance is the sister of patience. Perseverance is "continued, patient effort."

Perseverance is often the gift of the unsung hero, the one who quietly pushes on without fanfare or recognition. Helen Keller said, "I long to accomplish a great and noble task, but it is my chief duty to accomplish small tasks as if they were great and noble." We teach our children Aesop's fable about *The Tortoise and the Hare* and we tell them that "slow and steady wins the race," then we see others getting the stuff and the recognition that we would like to have and we forget our own advice. Going back to step 1 daily will help us remember.

We are results oriented. We are taught to be from an early age. As we work the steps, especially steps 9 and 12, "Making Amends and Giving it Away," we need to remember that the results are in God's hands, we are simply called to persevere, to "continued, patient effort." The Apostle Paul used a farming example to illustrate our part in recovery and discovery:

> "Who do you think Paul is, anyway? Or Apollos, for that matter? Servants, both of us—servants who waited on you as you gradually learned to entrust your lives to our mutual Master. We each carried out our servant assignment. I planted the seed, Apollos watered the plants, but *God* made you grow. It's not the one who plants or the one who waters who is at the center of this process but God, who makes things

grow. Planting and watering are menial servant jobs at minimum wages. What makes them worth doing is the God we are serving. You happen to be God's field in which we are working" (1 Corinthians 3:5–8, MSG).

Slow and steady wins the race to God and for God, not for us. For competing and comparing churches and denominations the essential question must be, "Who are we working and racing for?" As we work the steps, we need to avoid the trap that the institutional church has repeatedly fallen into.

Perseverance is a word seldom used in the Bible, but it has a synonym that is often used: endurance. Jesus said, "Sin will be rampant everywhere, and the love of many will grow cold. But the one who *endures* to the end will be saved" (Matthew 24:12–13, NLT, Jesus-Centered Bible). The author of the letter to the Hebrews urges us to "run with *endurance* the race that God has set before us ... keeping our eyes on Jesus" (Hebrews 12:1–2, NLT, Jesus-Centered Bible). Keep on keepin' on, working the steps is a marathon, not a sprint.

When we retired from the institutional church and started a new type of faith community called "follow" we looked around for a guide and discovered a book entitled *Called to Community: The Life Jesus Wants for His People*. This book is edited by Charles E. Moore and the contributors reads like a "who's who" of spiritual giants who have tried this thing called "intentional community," including Dietrich Bonhoffer, Joan Chittister, Dorothy Day, Richard Foster, Thomas Merton, Henri Nouwen, and Mother Teresa. The book is a "52-week journey ... once a week for a year."

The readings are not easy. The writers often challenge us to become very counter-cultural, to live and work in a way that is simple, non-competitive, and focused on the common good. Several times, we have been very tempted to skip readings, to move along faster, to race ahead, so that we can get busy being the community we envision. However, as we return to God and listen (step 11) daily, we have been reminded that slow and steady wins the race.

Patience, Persistence, Perseverance

Sisters and brothers, we're in this for the long haul. Keep on keepin' on. Keep working the steps … every hour of every day. Make recovery and discovery your lifestyle. Please know that we're all in this together, that we're praying for you, and that Jesus has our back.

Endnotes

[1.] William P. Young. *The Shack*, Windblown Media, 2007, page 274 (large print).

[2.] Hugh Halter and Matt Smay. *The Tangible Kingdom: Creating Incarnational Community*, Jossey-Bass, 2008.

[3.] Johann Hari, *Everything You Think you Know About Addiction is Wrong*, TED Talks, June 2015.

Going Deeper in Recovery and Discovery

Here are a few books that have helped us in our journey through recovery and discovery. We recommend that you include these books on your reading list.

Twelve-Step Programs

Big Book of Alcoholics Anonymous, Alcoholics Anonymous World Services (2001), 4th Edition
The original is still the best. The language can be difficult at times because it was first published in 1939, but the message and the process are timeless.

Twelve Steps and Twelve Traditions, Narcotics Anonymous World Services (2008), 6th Edition
Broader application, updated language, more stories, and helpful hints from practitioners.

Church

Church Refugees, Josh Packard and Ashley Hope, Group Publishing, Loveland, CO (2015)
Groundbreaking research. Sociologists reveal why people are leaving the institutional church in unprecedented numbers and identify a new spiritual demographic, the DONES.

Jesus Insurgency: The Church Revolution from the Edge, Dottie Escobedo-Frank and Rudy Rasmus, Abingdon Press, Nashville (2011)
Changing the church from the outside in. The institution will never change of its own accord. Speaks truth to power from those on the fringe and those ministering to them.

Spirituality

The Shack, William P. Young, Windblown Media (2007)
"This book has the potential to do for our generation what John Bunyan's *Pilgrim's Progress* did for his. It's that good!" (Eugene Peterson).

The Jesus-Centered Life, Rick Lawrence, Group Publishing (2016)
Moving Jesus from top priority in life to the center of life and falling in love with Jesus all over again.

Bridges between Addiction and Spirituality

Addiction and Grace: Love and Spirituality in the Healing of Addictions,
Gerald G. May, MD, HarperCollins Publishers, (1988)
A classic. This book will help you connect the dots that you always knew were there.

Breathing Under Water: Spirituality and the Twelve Steps, Richard Rohr,
St. Anthony Messenger Press, (2011)
Deep and rich. Contemplative, holistic approach to discovering the God that lives in each of us, no matter what.

About the Authors

Gerri Harvill and Stan Norman are co-leaders of "follow: a community," a group of Jesus-followers who meet in cafes and homes in Sandpoint, Idaho. Gerri and Stan both had successful secular careers before becoming professional clergy. Gerri was a dental assistant and project manager for a manufacturing firm. Stan is a retired US Coast Guard officer and Washington State environmental program manager. He is an ordained elder in the United Methodist Church. He holds a master of divinity degree from Fuller Theological Seminary. Gerri is a United Methodist licensed local pastor who studied at St. Paul School of Theology in Kansas City. Stan and Gerri are retired pastors who have chosen to step outside the institution of the church to discover what it means to simply follow Jesus.